Forever in Love

Devotional Insights for
Developing Love and
Intimacy in Your Marriage

by

Richard Exley

Tulsa, Oklahoma

Forever in Love
Devotional Insights for Developing Love and Intimacy in Your Marriage
ISBN 1-58919-288-5
Copyright ©1997 by Richard Exley
P. O. Box 57444
Tulsa, Oklahoma 74155

Published by River Oak
P. O. Box 55388
Tulsa, Oklahoma 74155

For *Brenda Starr.*

My favorite person in all the world,

and the co-author of my most important work — life.

Contents

Preface

Forever in Love is designed to help you and your spouse experience all that your marriage can be. To achieve the maximum benefit, I would like to suggest that you read one chapter each day, out loud with your spouse, and complete the "Love in Action" step. This will enable you to integrate the marriage principles into your own relationship.

While each chapter stands alone, they find their fullest meaning only in the context of the entire book. Each one is like a snapshot that captures a particular moment in marriage, but only a moment. In order to fully appreciate each singular moment, it is necessary to see them in relationship with all the rest. Viewed as a whole, it is possible to see how love redeems our differences, transcends our selfishness, and ultimately makes us one.

Remember, "House and wealth are inherited from parents, but a prudent wife (or husband) is from the Lord."[1]

Richard Exley

chapter 1

People Can Change, Can't They?

*A*s a minister I do a considerable amount of pre-marriage counseling. In the course of these sessions I inevitably ask each couple, "What do you like least about your fianceé? What habits does he/she have that get on your nerves?" As you might imagine, most engaged couples are uncomfortable with this line of questioning. They would rather talk about each other's good points.

I press them, and the tension mounts. He looks at her. She looks at him. They both look back at me. Silently, I wait with a half smile on my lips. Finally, she breaks the silence and divulges something, all the while being careful not to look at him. His face usually turns red, and he squirms uncomfortably in his chair.

"Do you think," I ask her, straight-faced, "that you can live with that for the next fifty years?"

Defensively, she responds, "People can change, can't they?"

Turning to him I ask, "Did you hear what she said?"

He looks puzzled, but replies, "She said people can change, can't they?"

"That's the words she used, but that's not what she said. She said that she has no intention of living with you the way you are. As soon as you two are married, she's going to remake you into the man she thinks you ought to be."

He looks at her incredulously, "Is that what you said?"

"Not really," she explains nervously. "I mean, it sounds so crass when you put it that way." Gathering her courage, she plunges ahead. "Surely you'll outgrow your bad habits."

A wise man would probably call the whole wedding off right there, but then wisdom is not a virtue very often found in young, engaged men. Instead, he listens intently while I tell her that anything that bothers her during courtship will drive her absolutely mad after they marry. I explain that people do mature, and the maturing process does bring about change, but those changes seldom affect a person's annoying habits. She nods wisely, and he assumes she has made peace with his idiosyncrasies. I know better. Even while we speak, she is plotting her post-wedding strategy.

This situation may seem amusing, but in real life it is an altogether different matter. As one wife said a year after the wedding, "During the engagement I was so afraid of losing him that, although I noticed a lot of things I did not like, I didn't say anything. I thought things would get better after the wedding. Now all we do is fight."

What is the source of this conflict — his behavior or her demands? That depends on the individual situation, of course, but more often than not it is her demands. When he doesn't meet them, she experiences anger. What she fails to realize is that the source of her anger and frustration is her demands, not her spouse's behavior.

This very behavior, the thing that is apparently driving her to despair, is not a new thing. It is not infidelity, or domestic violence, or alcohol abuse. It is an annoying habit, like eating with his mouth open, nothing more. It was present during their courtship, and it did not make her angry then. Why? Because she did not demand that he change. It is the frustration of her demands then, not his behavior, that is the source of her anger.

The quickest way to resolve this dilemma and restore peace in the relationship is for her to release her demands and accept him unconditionally, the way she did during their courtship. If change is really important to her, she should make it a matter of prayer. After all, only God can change another person. And when she prays, let her also ask God to change her, to make her the kind of wife He has called her to be.

♡ Love in Action

Make a list of the habits each of you would like your spouse to change. Now prayerfully eliminate any item that is not really essential to your happiness and well-being. Then approach one another in a new manner, such as: "I would appreciate it if you would..." or, "I would really prefer that you...." Once you have shared your concerns with each other in this manner, leave them in God's hands.

♡ Thought for the Day

"I really married my wife because of her difference. It is not my job to make her over, but rather to discover and value that difference."[1]

— Abraham Schmitt

♡ Scripture for the Day

"For this reason a man will leave his father and mother and be united to his wife, and the two will become one flesh." This is a profound mystery — but I am talking about Christ and the church. However, each one of you also must love his wife as he loves himself, and the wife must respect her husband.

— Ephesians 5:31-33

♡ *Prayer*

Lord, love is not demanding. Therefore, when I demand that my spouse change to please me, I am not acting in love regardless of how much I protest to the contrary. Forgive my arrogance. In Your holy name I pray. Amen.

chapter 2

♡ ♡ ♡ ♡

Gary's Girl

*O*n the eve of her wedding, a young woman received a letter from her father, in which he wrote:

"After tomorrow you will be Gary's wife. Our daughter still, but not in the same way, not ever again. From the moment the minister pronounces you husband and wife, your first allegiance, your first loyalty, will belong to Gary. Our home will no longer be your home. With Gary you will now make a new home of your own. You must leave us emotionally before you can cleave to your husband, before you can truly become one flesh with him.

"This does not mean that you are no longer in relationship with your mother and me, only that our relationship has changed. Whereas, before, it was 'the' primary relationship, it has now become a secondary one. Still important, to be sure, but not as important. Now the husband-wife relationship is preeminent. Under God, your relationship with your husband must be the most important relationship in all your life.

"If your marriage is good, you can overcome anything — financial adversity, illness, rejection, anything. If it is not good, there is not enough success in the world to fill the awful void. Absolutely nothing is more important than your marriage, so work at it with love and thoughtfulness all the days of your life.

"Guard it against all intruders. Remember your vows. You have promised, before God and your families, to forsake all others and cleave only to each other. Never allow friends, or family, or work, or anything else to come between you and your beloved.

"Marriage is made of time, so schedule time together. Spend it wisely in deep sharing. Tell him your whole heart. Listen carefully and with understanding when he in turn shares his heart with you. Spend it wisely in fun — laugh and play together. Go places and do things together. Spend it wisely in worship — pray together. Spend it wisely in touching — hold each other — be affectionate.

"Remember, a song isn't a song until you sing it, a bell isn't a bell until you ring it, and love isn't love until you give it away, so give all of your love to each other all the days of your life."

♡♡ *Love in Action*

Ask your spouse if you are putting anyone or anything ahead of him/her in your life. If the answer is yes, ask him/her to help you make whatever changes are necessary to make him/her number one in your life.

♡♡ *Thought for the Day*

"Bonding [is] the emotional covenant that links a man and woman together for life. It is the specialness which sets those two lovers apart from every other person on the face of the earth."[1]

— Dr. Desmond Morris

♡♡ *Scripture for the Day*

His heart was drawn to Dinah daughter of Jacob, and he loved the girl and spoke tenderly to her.

— Genesis 34:3

♡♡ *Prayer*

Lord, bind our hearts together in love. May we never allow anything to come between us — not family or friends, nor work or pleasure. In Your holy name I pray. Amen.

chapter 3
♡ ♡ ♡ ♡

A Marriage Made in Heaven

The groom is striking in his dark tuxedo, tall and slim, the oldest son of a minister. The bride, the youngest of five children, is radiant in a traditional white wedding gown. Everyone says that theirs is a "marriage made in heaven," and the future could not look brighter.

At first glance they seem an ideal match. They share the same church background, come from similar socioeconomic levels, and are compatible in their interests and education. He plans on entering the ministry, and she dreams of being a minister's wife. Yet, five short years later their marriage is just a bitter memory, a divorce statistic.

What happened?

Too soon they discovered that they were not prepared for the pressure of living together day after day. Their starry-eyed romanticism was simply no match for the reality of a one-bedroom apartment, an unbelievably tight budget, and the irritating habits of a spouse who can only be described as insensitive.

They might have overcome all of that, as many couples do, had it not been for their fatal belief in the myth about marriages being "made in heaven." That's the one that says, "If you marry the person God has chosen to be your mate, you will live happily ever after."

Couples who embrace this myth run at least two risks. First, they are tempted to take their marriage for granted. They mistakenly believe that since it was made in heaven it will be great without any special effort on their part. Of course, this results in a less than perfect marriage, which leads to the second temptation. Once the marriage starts to fall apart, it is easy for each of them to conclude that they married the wrong person and thus the marriage is doomed to failure.

While marrying God's chosen mate does not guarantee a good marriage, neither does marrying the "wrong person" mean that a miserable marriage is inevitable.

Once a couple marries, all thoughts about the rightness or wrongness of their choice should be put out of their minds. If they will both commit themselves to God and to the marriage, they can have a fulfilling relationship even if they married the "wrong person."

Good marriages don't just happen, not even when each individual marries "the right person." They are the product of the combined efforts of God and two committed people who have chosen to make their marriage a high priority, who have each decided that their spouse's happiness is more important than their own, and who have determined that nothing will be allowed to undermine their relationship.

♡ *Love in Action*

Make an unconditional commitment to your marriage right now. Determine that, with God's help, you will make your marriage all it can be. List some specific ways in which you will live out your renewed commitment to your marriage.

♡ *Thought for the Day*

"Marriage may be 'made in heaven' in the original. But the whole deal is more like one of those kits which comes knocked down for putting together. It will take some gluing here, sanding rough spots there, hammering a bit now, filing down the scratches on this side, planing a bit on that side, carving a piece, bending this section slightly, varnishing, backing off for a frequent look, dusting, waxing, polishing, until at last what you have is a thing of beauty and a joy forever."[1]

— Charlie W. Shedd

♡ *Scripture for the Day*

Houses and wealth are inherited from parents, but a prudent wife [or husband] is from the LORD.

— Proverbs 19:14

♡♡ *Prayer*

Lord, I have to confess that I often put unrealistic expectations on my spouse. I expect him/her to make me happy. I expect him/her to understand my needs when I can't even put them into words myself. I expect him/her to always respond to my personal needs or desires no matter what is going on in his/her life. I expect too much! Help me to make up for all the times I've made him/her feel inadequate by expecting him/her to do what only You can do. In Jesus' name I pray. Amen.

chapter 4

♡ ♡ ♡ ♡

Real Men Don't Eat Malt-o-Meal

*B*renda sits on the edge of the bed coaxing me into wakefulness, and as sleep flees it all comes rushing back — the wedding, our first night together at the historic Warwick Hotel in Houston, and breakfast in our room. There was linen napkins, real china and silver, and a single red rose in a crystal vase. That was the extent of our honeymoon; it was all we could afford, just one extravagant night in the Warwick, but it was worth every penny it cost.

Now it is over, and we are in our own little apartment beginning our first day of real marriage.

"You look wonderful," I say, rubbing sleep from my eyes. And she does. Her dark brown hair is brushed, and she has put on make-up. I experience a moment of gratefulness as I think of spending the rest of my life with this beautiful woman.

Grabbing my hand she says playfully, "Get up, lazybones. I've made you breakfast, but I'm not going to serve you in bed."

I'm not sure what I expected, bacon and eggs maybe, with a cup of steaming black coffee. After all, that's what Mom made for my dad. What I didn't expect was a candlelit breakfast served on china.

Trying to appear nonchalant, I take my seat and survey the table. "What's this?" I ask, pointing at a cereal bowl containing a foreign-looking substance.

There must have been something in the tone of my voice because Brenda gives me a hurt look before she replies. "That's Malt-o-Meal. It's my dad's favorite."

"Malt-o-Meal," I say, not even trying to hide my disgust. "Real men don't eat Malt-o-Meal."

Brenda is more than a little peeved, but she makes a valiant effort to remain calm. "Well, at least have some toast," she says, offering me a slice.

Trying to be civil myself, I smile thinly and take a piece, only to be blind-sided again. "What kind of toast is this?" I demand. "It's only toasted on one side, for heaven's sake!"

"It's oven toast," she replies through gritted teeth, "and if you don't like it you don't have to eat it."

Without another word I leave the table and head for the shower. Slamming the bathroom door, I lean against the wall muttering to myself. "Malt-o-Meal and one-sided toast," I fume, "what kind of breakfast is that?"

What we have here is a classic example of newlywed bliss falling prey to immaturity and the reality of marriage.

Without realizing it, I expected Brenda to be like my mother. At least I expected her to cook breakfast the way my mother did. For her part, Brenda expected me to be like her father, at least in the things I liked to eat.

Like many newlyweds, we discovered we had distinctly different models for marriage. Although both of us were reared in a Christian family with the same basic values, there were still many individual differences — differences that put no little strain on our young marriage. The challenge for us, and for most newlyweds, was to give up our parental models for marriage and together develop one that was uniquely our own.

♥ *Love in Action*

Examine your marriage to see if you have developed a model that is uniquely suited for the two of you. If you are still clinging to your parental models of marriage, decide together what changes you would like to make.

♥ *Thought for the Day*

"The bride and groom have successfully left home. They're on their own. But the home has not left them.

"The old patterns from home color nearly everything in the new marriage. Do you open gifts on Christmas Eve or Christmas morning? Do you make your bed immediately upon rising or when you go through the house tidying up? The way

you did it when you were growing up is right, of course. Any other way, though not exactly wrong, isn't right either."[1]

— Dr. Frank and Mary Alice Minirth

— Dr. Brian and Dr. Deborah Newman

— Dr. Robert and Susan Hemfelt

♡♡ Scripture for the Day

For this reason a man will leave his father and mother and be united to his wife, and they will become one flesh.

— Genesis 2:24

♡♡ Prayer

Lord, I can't believe how selfish and immature I can be at times. Change me. Help me become the kind of spouse that I should be. In the name of Jesus I pray. Amen.

chapter 5

Who's Going to Make the Coffee?

I grew up in a home where coffee is serious business. The first thing Mother did when she got up in the morning was go to the kitchen and get the coffee maker going. Then she started breakfast. By the time my father entered the kitchen, after finishing his shower and dressing for work, there was a steaming cup of that dark brew waiting for him. Of course, I expected Brenda to follow in Mom's footsteps.

Wrong! Brenda's parents didn't drink coffee. Consequently, she never developed a taste for it. As far as she was concerned, coffee was not part of the marriage vows. To her way of thinking, he who drinks the coffee should also make it. And clean up the mess, I might add.

There's more, lots more. Not only was the Wallace household a coffee-free zone, but they ate only one family meal a day. The rest of the time it was everyone for himself. At our house, we ate three meals a day, and by the clock. Imagine my dismay when Brenda informed me that she would be preparing only one meal each day. To make matters worse, there wouldn't be a scheduled mealtime either. She was the cook, and she would cook when it best suited her schedule.

Then there was the matter of Sunday breakfast. Growing up, Brenda seldom ate breakfast, and never on Sunday. For me, it was a family tradition. We usually had my brother Don's favorite, which was French toast and sausage, or Dad's — biscuits and gravy.

I tried to explain this to Brenda, but it was no use. Patiently she told me that there was absolutely no way she could cook breakfast and still be ready for church on time. At this point I made a near-fatal mistake. I pointed out that my mother had herself and four children to get ready for church, yet she still managed to fix a wonderful breakfast each Sunday.

Giving me a look that could kill, Brenda said sweetly, "Well, I'm not your mother."

The issues we're talking about aren't really big things. They do, however, illustrate the kind of adjustments almost all couples face in the early days of their marriage. How they handle these housekeeping items will go a long way toward determining the emotional climate of their relationship.

There are three basic ways to resolve any conflict: 1) compromise, 2) agree to disagree, 3) give in. Finding the right solution to a particular conflict is one of the keys to developing a fulfilling marriage.

Of course, different situations demand different solutions. In the case of daily meals, Brenda and I compromised. We now have two meals a day. When we eat them is flexible, depending on our schedules.

We never eat breakfast on Sundays. On this point I gave in; not grudgingly, but with good humor. Being a pastor, I decided it was more important to have an attractive wife at my side on Sunday mornings than to have a full stomach.

About the coffee, we agreed to disagree. I still think Brenda should make it, and she still thinks it's my responsibility. Generally, I brew my own coffee, but from time to time Brenda surprises me with a steaming cup of espresso. When she does, I feel especially loved.

On issues like these, there really isn't a right way or a wrong way. Rather, each couple must work out a system that is best for them. The sooner they do so, the sooner they can move on to more important things.

♡ *Love in Action*

Make a list of the unresolved issues in your marriage. How many of them are worth fighting about? Will it really matter five years from now, or ten? With God's help determine how you are going to resolve them.

♡ *Thought for the Day*

"Marriage immediately forces changes upon the partners which, no matter how well prepared they thought they were,

surprise them and require a new and specialized labor from both of them. This is the fact: the woman does not know who her husband is until he is her husband, nor the man his wife until she exists as wife. Before the marriage these people were fiancées, not spouses; fiancées and spouses are different creatures, and the second creature doesn't appear until the first has passed away. Did the courtship last many, many years? It doesn't matter. Were they friends long before they initiated courtship? It doesn't matter. They still can't know the spouse until he or she is a spouse; and there isn't a spouse until there is a marriage.

"So the recently married couple has a job to do, a good job, a hopeful and rewarding job, but labor nonetheless. And it will take a patient, gentle energy to accomplish this labor well."[1]

— Walter Wangerin, Jr.

♡♡ *Scripture for the Day*

Do nothing out of selfish ambition or vain conceit, but in humility consider others better than yourselves. Each of you should look not only to your own interests, but also to the interests of others.

— Philippians 2:3,4

♡♡ *Prayer*

Lord, it is so easy to assume that "our" way is the only way. Forgive us. Help each of us to be more understanding, more willing to compromise. In the name of Jesus we pray. Amen.

chapter 6

♡ ♡ ♡ ♡

Wedding Vows and Dirty Clothes

"Will you please come into the bathroom and put your dirty clothes in the hamper," Brenda calls, with just a hint of impatience in her voice.

I am in the living room of our small apartment, preparing a sermon for tonight's service. The last thing I want to do is interrupt my sermon preparation, especially for something so mundane.

"I'm busy, sweetheart," I call in my most persuasive voice. "Could you do it for me this one time?"

"I'm not your maid," Brenda replies, "and I'm not going to pick up after you. You are perfectly capable of putting your own clothes in the hamper."

Slamming my Bible down on the coffee table, I march into the bathroom. We've hardly been married a week and already our happy home is going up in smoke. It is time, I reason, to put my foot down before things really get out of hand.

"Brenda," I ask, "can you remember where we were ten days ago?"

Without giving her a chance to reply, I plunge ahead.

"Let me refresh your memory. It was the evening of June tenth, in the year of our Lord nineteen hundred and sixty-six. We were in Central Assembly of God reciting our wedding vows. As you can probably recall, you were standing before our pastor, the Rev. W. A. Majors, vowing a number of holy promises, both to me and to God."

Looking at me like I've lost my mind, she asks, "What does that have to do with putting your dirty clothes in the hamper?"

"Everything," I reply. "Absolutely everything! In the presence of our families and friends, you vowed to forsake all others and cleave only to me. Not only did you pledge to love me, for better or worse, for richer or poorer, in sickness or in health, till death do us part, but you also promised to obey me!"

Drawing myself up to my full height of five feet nine inches, I deliver the coup de grace.

"Pick up my clothes," I order in my most authoritarian voice, "and put them in the hamper."

Without a word, Brenda walks out of the bathroom, leaving me sucking air like a pump out of water.

When we moved out of that apartment six weeks later, my dirty clothes were still behind the bathroom door. (I'm just kidding.)

After pouting for most of the afternoon, I finally swallowed my pride and did what I should have done in the first place — I put my dirty clothes in the hamper.

You may be wondering why I am recounting such a silly experience. Precisely for that reason — because it is so silly. Like many of the things couples fight about, it is absolutely hilarious in retrospect. Next time you are tempted to fight with your spouse, ask yourself if the issue is really worth fighting over. Chances are it's not.

♡ *Love in Action*

Together with your spouse examine the things you usually fight about. Will those issues really matter five years from now? Or even six months from now? If they won't, then they are not worth fighting about. Determine together that you will stop fighting over insignificant things.

♡ *Thought for the Day*

Never burn down the house to get rid of your mice.[1]

— Charlie W. Shedd

♡ *Scripture for the Day*

He who guards his lips guards his life, but he who speaks rashly will come to ruin.... A gentle answer turns away wrath, but a harsh word stirs up anger.

— Proverbs 13:3; 15:1

♡♡ *Prayer*

Lord, set a watch over my lips. Let no angry word come from my mouth. Teach me to speak the truth in love. In the name of Jesus I pray. Amen.

chapter 7

♡ ♡ ♡ ♡

Charlie Shedd's Folly

*W*hen I was just nineteen years old and in my first year of Bible college, I was privileged to hear Charlie Shedd speak in chapel. Not only was he a successful pastor, but a best-selling author as well, having written several books, including Letters to Karen[1], and Letters to Philip[2]. Since I was planning to be married in a few weeks, and he was best known for his books on marriage, I hung on his every word.

About money he said, "Give 10 percent, save 10 percent, and spend the rest with thanksgiving." About the family he said, "Wherever Dad sits is the head of the table." There's more, but the thing I remember best is what he said about keeping the home fires burning. With a twinkle in his eye, he counseled us young ministers, "No matter how financially strapped you may be, always buy your wife a beautiful negligee at least once a year."

A few weeks later, Brenda and I were married. About eighteen months thereafter I accepted the call to be the pastor of a small church in rural Colorado. It was a challenging situation, to say the least. Sunday morning attendance averaged less than thirty people, counting the children. And we were, in Charlie Shedd's words, strapped! Our total income that first year was barely twenty-six hundred dollars. Still, I managed to buy Brenda a beautiful nightgown that year, and each of the following three years.

Imagine my surprise when she became tearfully angry upon receiving her fourth nightgown in as many years. Throwing it on the bed, she said, "All you ever buy me are negligees. And it's not even for me, not really."

"What do you mean, it's not for you?" I demanded, more confused than angry.

"It's for you," she said. "I'm supposed to put it on and look sexy — for you, for your pleasure. Then we'll make love, and I'll feel used. Just once I wish you would buy me a new dress."

If I could have gotten my hands on Charlie Shedd, I would have strangled him. Still, after I had time cool off, I began to understand where Brenda was coming from.

The issue wasn't just a new dress, though that would have been nice. What Brenda wanted, and needed, was a public demonstration of my love — something that said to the world, "I love this woman. I'm glad she's my wife."

A new dress is not the only way to do that, and not necessarily the best way. Belatedly, I discovered the importance of small gestures of affection, like holding her hand in public, or taking her arm as we crossed the street. These made her feel special, as did a timely compliment. And feeling special is an important part of love, especially to a woman.

I will probably never fully fathom the mystery of the feminine mind, nor will any other man, not even Charlie Shedd or Dr. James Dobson. Still, if I can remember to love Brenda in ways that make her feel loved, rather than in ways that make me feel loving, things will turn out all right more often than not.

♡ *Love in Action*

Ask your spouse what you do that makes him/her feel loved. Take special note of the things your spouse mentions and make it a point to do at least one of them every day.

♡ *Thought for the Day*

I was blown away when I first learned that [being thoughtful and attentive was high on my wife's list of the ways of expressing love]. It meant that if I wanted to express my love and care in a way that was important to her, a simple act like opening the car door would do it.[3]

— Rich Buhler

♥ Scripture for the Day

This is how we know what love is: Jesus Christ laid down his life for us. And we ought to lay down our lives for our brothers. If anyone has material possessions and sees his brother in need but has no pity on him, how can the love of God be in him? Dear children, let us not love with words or tongue but with actions and in truth.

— 1 John 3:16-18

♥ Prayer

Lord, enable me to express my love in ways that are meaningful to my spouse. In the name of Jesus I pray. Amen.

chapter 8

♡ ♡ ♡

I Love You

Too many men, I'm afraid, are like the elderly Vermont man who was reared to believe that silence was eternally golden. One night he and his wife were rocking silently, side by side, when he muttered painfully, "Sometimes, Maudy, I love you so much it's almost more than I can do not to tell you."[1]

That would be funny if it weren't so tragic. And it's not as far-fetched as you might think. You would be absolutely amazed at the number of men who find it nearly impossible to say, "I love you." Then again, maybe you wouldn't. At least, not if you are married to one of those men who have been described as the strong, silent type.

I once counseled with a couple who were at odds over this very issue. The wife was hurting. She was feeling lonely and insecure. Distinctly I remember her saying to her husband, "You haven't told me you love me since the night you proposed."

Disgruntled, he replied, "Well, nothing's changed, and when it does you'll be the first to know."

Unfortunately, his insensitive reply did little to warm their rapidly cooling relationship.

Another equally silent type told his wife, "Of course I love you. I make a good living for you and the kids, don't I?"

Indeed he did, and his wife was grateful, but she needed more than his paycheck to feel loved. Deeds may suffice for most men, but women need words as well as deeds to assure them they are loved and appreciated.

According to Dr. James Dobson, "...genuine love is a fragile flower. It must be maintained and protected if it is to survive. Love can perish...when there is no time for romantic activity...when a man and his wife forget how to talk to each other."[2]

♡♡ *Love in Action*

Determine right now that at least once a day you are going to tell your spouse that you love him/her. As a special gesture, sit down and write him/her a love letter.

♡♡ *Thought for the Day*

"Speaking and doing are two sides of a single coin. Only the word clarifies beyond doubt the great mystery of love's motivation behind the acts that make life smooth. Only the word carries the constant reminder in the doldrums of mundane activity; only the word sings in the ear and repeats itself in the memory."[3]

— Dorothy T. Samuel

♡♡ *Scripture for the Day*

Many women do noble things, but you surpass them all. Charm is deceptive, and beauty is fleeting; but a woman who fears the LORD is to be praised. Give her the reward she has earned, and let her works bring her praise at the city gate.

— Proverbs 31:29-31

♡♡ *Prayer*

Lord, teach me to love in both word and deed. In Your holy name I pray. Amen.

chapter 9

My Dog's Better Than Your Dog

*I*t is February 1967, and we are in Rapid City, South Dakota. There is two feet of snow on the ground, and the temperature is hovering right at twenty degrees below zero. (That's the actual temperature, not the wind chill. In fact, if my memory serves me right, no one was even figuring wind chill factors in the sixties.)

Brenda and I are newly married and preaching revival meetings in little churches from Cuero, Texas to Post Falls, Idaho, and a half a hundred places in between. It is a great way to make memories, but not something I would like to do again. In most places we stay with the local pastor and his family. Usually we displace one of the children, making their cramped bedroom our own for the duration of the scheduled services.

As is often the case, the parsonage in Rapid City is small, with only one bathroom. To expedite matters, Brenda is bathing while I stand at the sink shaving. Soon she begins to sing. But she does not sing one of the great hymns of the

Church, nor even a praise chorus. Neither does she sing a romantic ballad or even a love song. No, Brenda is singing a commercial jingle!

"My dog's better than your dog, my dog's better than yours.

My dog's better 'cause he eats Kennel Ration.

My dog's better than yours."

Brenda has a lovely voice, not unlike the late Karen Carpenter's, and I love to hear her sing, but a man can only take so much of the "Kennel Ration" song. After listening to her sing about her dog being better, bigger, faster, smarter, and prettier, I can bear no more.

Kindly I ask Brenda to please stop singing that song. Smiling warmly she agrees, and I turn back to my shaving. I have hardly raised my razor before she belts it out again. Turning from the sink I glare at her.

"Oops!" she says.

Once more I resume my shaving only to be blind-sided again. Picking up a large glass from the bathroom counter, I fill it to the brim with frigid tap water.

"Brenda," I say, not even attempting to disguise my irritation, "if you don't stop singing that stupid song I'm going to douse you with cold water."

Brenda is a lovely lady, sweet and genteel, but underneath she is as tough as nails and nobody intimidates her.

Defiantly she lifts her chin and begins to sing — "My dog's better than your dog...."

I let her have it. And in an instant she is gasping for breath, stunned by a glass of water whose temperature is just above freezing.

She's stubborn, I'll give her that — but not very smart. As soon as she can catch her breath, she starts to sing again. I don't want to do it, but I have no choice. Reluctantly I refill the glass and douse her again.

Same result.

By now her teeth are chattering, and she is visibly shivering. In amazement, I watch as she gathers herself, and through clenched teeth sings, "My dog's better than your dog...."

Her absolute defiance destroys the last of my sympathy. Angrily I turn back to the sink and refill the glass for the third time. With sadistic delight I let her have it one more time.

This time she stays down for the count, but I am the loser. I have won the argument, but I have lost what is most precious to me — Brenda's companionship. I tell you the truth, and I do not exaggerate. Spring came and went before the temperature ever got above freezing in our bedroom.

Was it worth it? Hardly. The victories we "win" in our marital conflicts seldom are, for it is not an enemy we vanquish, but the love of our life.

♡ *Love in Action*

Take some time with your spouse and discuss the role that conflict plays in your marriage. Is it constructive or destructive? How can it be better handled? Be specific.

♡ *Thought for the Day*

"I would say to all: use your gentlest voice at home."

— Anonymous

♡ *Scripture for the Day*

Do not let any unwholesome talk come out of your mouths, but only what is helpful for building others up according to their needs, that it may benefit those who listen.

— Ephesians 4:29

♡ *Prayer*

Lord, we have sinned against our marriage. Forgive us. Restore our relationship. Heal the hurts we have inflicted on each other. In Your holy name we pray. Amen.

chapter 10

♡ ♡ ♡ ♡

The Box

*A*n African myth tells of a tribe whose people noticed that their cows were not giving as much milk as they once did. After consulting among themselves, they decided someone must be stealing their milk. That night they posted a watch. About midnight the watchman noticed a beautiful young woman floating down to earth on a moon beam. Like a shadow she moved from cow to cow, stealing a little milk from each one. When her pail was finally filled, she went back to the skies.

She returned again the next night only to be trapped by the watchman, who discovered that she was the Sky Maiden, a member of a sky tribe who had no other way to get food for themselves. Being beautiful, she immediately won his heart, and he agreed to release her if she would marry him. She consented, but only on the condition that he would allow her to return to the sky for three days and prepare herself.

Returning to earth, she brought with her a large sealed box. Following the wedding, she made her husband promise he would never open it. They lived happily together until the bridegroom's curiosity got the best of him. Finally he could stand it no more, and one day when his wife was away from their hut, he opened the box and looked inside. To his amazement he discovered it was empty.

When she returned to the hut, the Sky Maid realized that he had looked inside the box. To his distress, she refused to be married to him any longer. He could not understand why she would leave him over something as trivial as an empty box.

"I'm not leaving you because you opened the box," she explained, "I thought you probably would. I'm leaving you because you said it was empty. It wasn't empty; it was full of sky. It contained the light and the air and the smells of my home in the sky. When I went home for the last time, I filled that box with everything that was most precious to me to remind me of where I came from. How can I be your wife if what is most precious to me is emptiness to you?"[1]

The moral of this myth should be obvious. A man cannot truly love his spouse if what is most precious to her is nothing to him.

♥ *Love in Action*

Take whatever steps are necessary to know your spouse in order to love him/her. Make sure you know what your spouse's greatest concern is right now. What his/her greatest need is. What his/her wildest dream is. What his/her smallest pain is.

♡♡ *Thought for the Day*

"...a Hasidic rabbi, renowned for his piety...was unexpectedly confronted one day by one of his devoted youthful disciples. In a burst of feeling, the young disciple exclaimed, 'My master, I love you!' The ancient teacher looked up from his books and asked his fervent disciple, 'Do you know what hurts me, my son?'

The young man was puzzled. Composing himself, he stuttered, 'I don't understand your question, Rabbi. I am trying to tell you how much you mean to me, and you confuse me with irrelevant questions.'

'My question is neither confusing nor irrelevant,' rejoined the rabbi, 'for if you do not know what hurts me, how can you truly love me?'"[2]

— Madeleine L'Engle

♡♡ *Scripture for the Day*

...show me your face, let me hear your voice; for your voice is sweet, and your face is lovely.

— Song of Songs 2:14

♡♡ *Prayer*

Lord, help me to be more sensitive, more in tune with my spouse's needs, and less concerned about my own. In the name of Jesus I pray. Amen.

chapter 11

Whose Man Are You?

*N*o man should have to choose between his wife and his mother, but inevitably all men must. Well do I remember the night it fell my lot. To the best of my knowledge it only happened once, and it was of my own doing.

Arriving at my parent's home, at about eleven o'clock one night, I announce that I am starved. Turning to Brenda, who is preparing our fifteen-month-old daughter for bed, I ask, "How about frying me a hamburger?"

Without looking up she replies, "It's late, and I need to put Leah to bed. Why don't you make yourself a sandwich?"

"Thanks a lot," I snap, making no attempt to keep the sarcasm out of my voice.

Ignoring my childish display of temper, Brenda picks Leah up and starts down the hall toward the bedroom.

"I'll fry you a hamburger," my mother volunteers. "Would you like one or two?"

Stopping dead in her tracks, Brenda spins on her heel and glares at my mother. Thankfully, Mom's back is turned so she does not see the look Brenda gives her, but I do. If looks could kill, my mother would be a dead woman!

Intuitively I realize this is a moment of truth for our young marriage. How I respond will set the course for our future. I am tempted to play dumb and enjoy my hamburger, but I decide against it.

Joining my mother in the kitchen, I put my arm around her shoulders. "Thanks, Mom," I say, "but I don't think I'm really hungry." Brushing her forehead with a goodnight kiss, I go to join Brenda and Leah in the guest room.

I watch from the doorway as Brenda finishes tucking Leah into bed. Glancing my direction, she asks snidely, "Aren't your hamburgers ready yet?"

Swallowing my anger, I cross the room and take her in my arms. I want to defend my mother I want to tell Brenda that Mom had no intention of offending her, but I don't. Instead, I hear myself saying, "I'm sorry, sweetheart. I wish Mom hadn't done that."

Not being a person given to many words, especially when she is angry, Brenda says nothing. Still, I sense her hurt. Although Mother was just being "Mom," Brenda feels put down, and well she might. Mom has invaded her territory, howbeit unintentionally. She has made her feel inadequate as a wife and homemaker.

By birth and blood I will always be my mother's son, but by love and marriage I am Brenda's husband first. With

God's help, I will do what must be done. Tonight, I will comfort my wife. I will absorb her anger without defending my mother. Tomorrow, I will speak to my mother. I will attempt to explain how Brenda feels. Hopefully, she will understand. The last thing I want to do is hurt her feelings. Still, if I must choose between Brenda's feelings and my mother's, then I will always choose Brenda's.

♡ *Love in Action*

Reaffirm your allegiance to your spouse, both verbally and in action. If you have been putting your parent's feelings ahead of your spouse's (e.g. in making holiday plans or deciding where you will spend your vacation) — stop! Make your plans together as a couple, putting your family's needs first.

♡ *Thought for the Day*

"Marriage is not so much finding the right person as it is being the right person!"[1]

— Charlie W. Shedd

♡ *Scripture for the Day*

...Where you go I will go, and where you stay I will stay. Your people will be my people and your God my God. Where you die I will die, and there I will be buried. May the LORD deal with me, be it ever so severely, if anything but death separates you and me.

— Ruth 1:16,17

♥ *Prayer*

Lord, forgive me for the times I have not been completely loyal to my spouse. Heal the wounds my disloyalty has caused. From this day forward help me to always put my spouse first in all I do. In Your holy name I pray. Amen.

chapter 12

♡ ♡ ♡ ♡

Savor the Joys of Today

"*O*ne of the most tragic things I know about human nature," said Dale Carnegie, "is that all of us tend to put off living. We are all dreaming of some magical rose garden over the horizon, instead of enjoying the roses that are blooming outside our windows today."[1]

Young couples are especially susceptible to this temptation. It is so easy to say, "Wait until we've saved enough money for a down payment on the house we want, and then we'll take a vacation." Then it's, "Once we get the house furnished, we'll take that trip we've been planning for so long." Or worse yet, they postpone happiness until some time in the future. "Once Jim gets his promotion, then we'll have some time together," or "I know things will be better between us once I'm able to quit working outside the home."

That's all well and good, but if you are really serious about making your marriage all God intends it to be, you are going to have to stop postponing life. Make the most of today, live it to the fullest — not recklessly or foolishly, but savoring every moment. The wise man wrote, "...rejoice in the wife of your youth, ...may her breasts satisfy you always, may you ever be captivated by her love."[2] Notice the emphasis on "always" and "ever."

I was reminded of how important it is to live every moment of our lives when I read, *A Legacy of Rainbows* by Aletha Jane Lindstrom. She tells of pausing beside a park fountain one spring morning to watch the spray diffuse sunlight into shimmering rainbows. While she enjoyed the moment, a young mother, followed by a tiny blond girl, came hurrying along the path. "When the child saw the fountain, she threw her arms wide. 'Mommy, wait!' she cried. 'See all the pretty colors!'

"The mother reached for her daughter's hand. 'Come on,' she urged. 'We'll miss our bus!' Then seeing the joy on the small face, she relented. 'All right,' she said. 'There'll be another bus soon.'

"As she knelt with her arms around the child, joy filled the mother's face too — that rare and special joy of sharing something lovely with someone we love."[3]

There are moments like that in marriage too, and it is a wise couple who takes time to pause in the rush of living to savor them. Sometimes it's something as simple as a few bars of an old song or an especially beautiful sunset. At other times it may be a poignant moment as you face a family crisis, such as a beloved parent's open-heart surgery, or the sorrow you share as you stand together beside the open grave of a loved one. Suddenly you know the true meaning of marriage, and you love each other so much you could cry.

♡ *Love in Action*

If you were to decide to live every moment to the fullest, what attitude adjustments would you have to make? What behavioral changes would be required? Be specific.

♡ *Thought for the Day*

"...the second memory is of the interior of our house when I happen to be home, once, and you are not. You've rearranged the furniture, and I stand gazing at the change you've made. I'm shaking my head. I'm shaking my head over you, astonished by your kindness. This house has two bedrooms; one is the children's, one is ours, and these are the only two rooms with doors and privacy. But here, in what used to be the sitting room, is all our bedroom furniture — and what used to be our bedroom has become a study, in which I am invited to write. Thanne! You've given up your bedroom. How can I answer that kind of love? I can't. I can only bow my head and stand in its light. And write."[4]

— Walter Wangerin, Jr.

♡ *Scripture for the Day*

How delightful is your love, my sister, my bride! How much more pleasing is your love than wine, and the fragrance of your perfume than any spice!

Your lips drop sweetness as the honeycomb, my bride; milk and honey are under your tongue."

— Song of Songs 4:10,11

♡ *Prayer*

Lord, yesterday has passed, and tomorrow may never come. This moment is all we have. Give us the wisdom and the courage to live it to the fullest. In the name of Jesus I pray. Amen.

chapter 13

Mars and Venus in the Bedroom

*I*f you have been married for any length of time, you have already discovered that you and your spouse are distinctly different sexual creatures. You may have even been tempted to wonder if there was something wrong with your spouse, or — God forbid — with yourself.

Stop worrying.

For reasons known only to God, men and women are created with different sexual needs and desires. As I am sure you have already found out, these differences can be a source of confusion, and even conflict. If they cannot be discussed and accommodated, they will inevitably undermine your sexual intimacy and have a negative impact on your marriage.

Some of the more obvious differences find expression in the varied ways men and women respond to the sex act itself.

A man can be quickly aroused to a climactic explosion, while a woman's sexual desires take time to build. Not infrequently, he is finished before she is hardly started. And when the moment of his supreme pleasure is over, he will be overcome with sleep, while she lies awake, staring at the ceiling. Let this happen a few times, and it is not difficult to understand why many young wives conclude that sex is vastly overrated.

It is a wise husband who teaches himself to be sensitive to his wife's needs and desires. With disciplined love he teaches his impatient body to wait until his wife has attained the same level of sexual arousal.

Even then, he does not demand a predetermined conclusion, but rather allows their lovemaking to create its own ending.

Although he must experience an orgasm in order to be satisfied, he has learned that there are times when his wife enjoys intercourse without the need for a climax. Even as he is sensitive to her need for complete fulfillment, he also honors her ability to experience pleasure without achieving an orgasm. He refuses to yield to the temptation to demand that she have an orgasm, or multiple orgasms, to prove his prowess as a lover.

Sex for a woman is a small part of a total package. She is attracted to the man who makes her feel attractive and special, loved and secure. When the emotional climate in their marriage is calm, when he spends time with her, when they do things together and share deeply, she finds herself in the mood for intimacy. In other words, her mind — what she is thinking — and her emotions — what she is feeling — play a significant role in her sexual desire.

While a man's emotions may affect his sexual performance, it is usually to a much lesser degree and often doesn't manifest itself until mid-life and beyond. In the early years of marriage, almost nothing dampens his desire — not job pressures, physical fatigue, or even marital quarrels — as many a young wife can attest.

Women are usually more concerned about propriety. The time and place have to be appropriate. They need privacy. They fear being overheard or interrupted. Of course, this can put considerable strain on the marriage.

Consider the young couple who spent their annual three-week vacation with her parents, who lived more than a thousand miles away. With wry humor he explains: "My wife couldn't imagine making love in her parents' home. What if they heard us? What if they knew what we were doing? Ultimately, she was able to overcome her inhibitions, but for a time it was a real source of tension between us."

It is critical that both partners recognize and accept their sexual differences. He is not some kind of sex maniac. She is not frigid. They are different, one from the other, and it is these very differences that challenge their love to grow.

As he subjugates his desires so he can meet hers, his love grows.

As she accommodates his needs, her love grows.

No longer is their sexuality a selfish thing, thinking only of its own fulfillment. Now it has been sanctified by their love, and it has become a way of expressing their spiritual and emotional connectedness.

♡♡ *Love in Action*

Not infrequently our sexual differences generate anger, causing us to say and do things that hurt our spouse. Take a few minutes and remember any of the hurtful things you may have said or done. Now apologize specifically for each one and seek your spouse's forgiveness.

♡♡ *Thought for the Day*

"If I had the power to communicate only one message to every family in America, I would specify the importance of romantic love to every aspect of feminine existence. It provides the foundation for a woman's self-esteem, her joy in living, and her sexual responsiveness."[1]

— Dr. James Dobson

♡♡ *Scripture for the Day*

The husband should fulfill his marital duty to his wife, and likewise the wife to her husband. The wife's body does not belong to her alone but also to her husband. In the same way, the husband's body does not belong to him alone but also to his wife. Do not deprive each other except by mutual consent and for a time, so that you may devote yourselves to prayer. Then come together again so that Satan will not tempt you because of your lack of self-control.

— 1 Corinthians 7:3-5

♡ *Prayer*

Lord, redeem my sexual desires. Make them a holy thing that I may use to love and serve my beloved. In the name of Jesus I pray. Amen.

chapter 14

♡ ♡ ♡

Intimacy is More Than Sex

*S*ome years ago Ann Landers wrote an article for *Family Circle* titled, "What 100,000 Women Told Ann Landers." In it she shared the results of a survey in which she asked her women readers: "Would you be content to be held close and treated tenderly and forget about 'the act'?"

Seventy-two percent of the respondents said yes, they would be content just to be held close and treated tenderly and forget about the sex act. Interestingly enough, 40 percent of those who said yes were under forty years of age.

Ann concluded: "...a great many women choose affection over sex. Those yes votes were saying, 'I want to be valued. I want to feel cared about. Tender words and loving embraces are more rewarding than an orgasm produced by a silent, mechanical, self-involved male.'"[1]

If you are a man, you may feel misunderstood or even threatened by that, but I hope not. My purpose for including it here is not to imply that men are insensitive creatures interested only in their own sexual fulfillment. My experience as a man, and as a minister who has counseled with hundreds of men, tells me that simply is not the case.

Granted, many husbands may appear to be one-dimensional in their marital relationship, but that is only because they have not learned to express their deepest feelings in non-sexual ways.

For a man, sex is a whole lot more than a physical act. It is his way of expressing his need for closeness, tenderness, and deep sharing. It is his heart's cry for intimacy. In truth, he experiences a haunting sadness when his wife contributes nothing more than her body. He may not be able to explain his need to her, but I can assure you, he hungers for emotional closeness as much as she does.

The real problem here is not sex, but communication. Both men and women make the mistake of assuming that their partner feels and responds the same way they do to the relational and emotional factors in their lives. This simply is not so.

When a woman feels lonely or depressed, the last thing she wants is sex. She wants her husband to hold her while she pours out the pain in her heart. She longs to be understood, to be comforted with non-sexual acts of affection, like a hug or a shared cup of tea. This, for her, is intimacy.

When a man feels alone or misunderstood, he doesn't want to talk about it. Indeed, he can't talk about it, for he has no words to express the pain he feels. Instead, he wants to make love with his wife. He wants to resolve his loneliness the only way he knows how — sexually. What he cannot express in words, he communicates in the force of his loving. This, for him, is intimacy.

In truth, true marital intimacy occurs on both the emotional and the physical level. It involves both talking and touching, both non-sexual and sexual acts of tenderness and affection.

Before Eve, Adam was alone, and it was not good. Although he shared a special relationship with all of God's creation, he was still alone in the deepest part of his soul. Even though he walked with God in the garden and communed with Him as friend with friend, there remained a part of him that was achingly alone.

The Scriptures declare: "...But for Adam no suitable helper was found."[2]

Where could he find his soul mate, that one who would finally end his aloneness? Not in the animal kingdom, for there was none like him. Nor in relationship with God, for that was intimacy on an altogether different plane. Only in marriage could he find the intimacy to satisfy his heart's hunger to know and be known. Only in marriage could he find the intimacy to satisfy his need for closeness and caring. Only in marriage could he find "flesh of his flesh and bone of his bone" to satisfy his need for sexual fulfillment.

So, "...the Lord God made a woman from the rib he had taken out of the man, and he brought her to the man.... The man and his wife were both naked, and they felt no shame."[3]

They were intimate; they had no secrets to hide from each other. They were fully known, each to the other, and they were not ashamed. They had a transparent relationship built on love and trust.

Because they were one, because they were truly bonded emotionally, they could give themselves to each other sexually without reservation. And because of their joyous and uninhibited physical union, their emotional intimacy was complete.

Without their blessed oneness, the physical act of making love would have been just that — a physical act — empty and unfulfilling. The merging of their flesh without the touching of their souls. That's loneliness of the most haunting kind. Yet, without the expression of their physical love, their emotional and spiritual intimacy would have been incomplete.

Marriage, as God meant it to be, brings it all together — the bread of love to nourish the spirit, the cup of forgiveness to wash our wounds and forgive our failures, to restore our blessed oneness. Nakedness that nothing need be hidden, transparency that we may at last know ourselves because finally we are known, and physical love that our aloneness might be swallowed up in the body of our beloved, that our love might give birth to a family.

In reality, what 100,000 women told Ann Landers is exactly what the Bible has been teaching for millenniums: Sex without intimacy is empty and unfulfilling.

♡♡ *Love in Action*

Briefly discuss ways in which you and your spouse can be more sensitive to each other in all areas, but especially as it relates to intimacy in marriage.

♡♡ *Thought for the Day*

"You never made
A lamp base out of a Cracker Jack box,
An extra room out of an unused closet,
Or a garden out of a pile of clay.
All you ever made was
A woman out of me."[4]

— Lois Wyse

♡♡ *Scripture for the Day*

Then David comforted his wife Bathsheba, and he went to her and lay with her....

— 2 Samuel 12:24

♡ *Prayer*

Lord, I thank You for the gift of marriage. There is nothing in all the world dearer than the intimacy I have found with my beloved. In the name of Jesus I pray. Amen.

chapter 15

♡ ♡ ♡ ♡

A Theology of Sex

What you believe about sex, or more particularly, what you believe the Bible says about sex, will have a profound influence on the sexual dimensions of your marriage. If you believe, as did one wife who sought my pastoral counsel, that sex is inherently evil, then you will experience tremendous difficulty enjoying the physically intimate aspects of marriage. Your marriage bed will be a stern place, inhabited by shame and guilt. And sex will be something to be endured, rather than enjoyed.

This same wife went on to confess that she feared her rather timid husband was unnatural in his sexual desires.

"What," I asked her, "do you mean by 'unnatural'?"

It wasn't easy for her to talk about these things, and she squirmed nervously in her chair before replying. Finally, she spoke, in an embarrassed tone. "He wants to see me when I have nothing on." Just telling me made her blush, but once the words were out she rushed on. "He doesn't think there is anything wrong with a husband and wife seeing each other naked. Sometimes he even asks me to let him come into the bathroom when I am bathing."

"There's one other thing," she continued, "but I don't know how to tell you." She fell silent, studying her nails intently, while chewing nervously on her lower lip. When I had just about given up hope that she would ever speak again, she closed her eyes, took a deep breath, and said, "He wants us to do it with the lights on — have sex, I mean — you know, make love. Sometimes he even wants to do it in the daytime."

Where, you may be wondering, did she get such a distorted view of sex? There are two primary sources: family and church. In a misdirected effort to counter the promiscuity that is rampant today, these authority figures sometimes give young people the wrong message. Instead of teaching that sex, within the bonds of holy matrimony, is a gift from God to be received with thanksgiving and celebrated without shame, they focus only on the sinful aspects of illicit sex. As a result, their children enter marriage with a faulty theology of sex.

Unlearning bad theology is never easy, but it can be done. Jesus said, '...you will know the truth, and the truth will set you free.'[1] What, then, is the truth about sex in marriage?

Sex was God's idea, and He called it good! "...male and female he created them. God blessed them and said to them, 'Be fruitful and increase in number....' God saw all that he had made, and it was very good...."[2]

Sex is a gift from God to be received with thanksgiving and celebrated without shame. It is designed to express love, cultivate intimacy, provide pleasure, and propagate the race. When God brought woman to man, they "...were both naked, and they felt no shame."[3]

The Scriptures teach that the marriage bed is "undefiled,"[4] which means that a husband and wife are free to discover the sexual expressions that are most pleasurable to each of them. Of course, anything that is physically or psychologically damaging to either partner is off-limits. Such acts are not love making, but exploitation.

I shared this information with the aforementioned wife. She listened intently, but was unable to conceal her skepticism, which shouldn't be surprising. A lifetime of erroneous teaching is not unlearned in a single afternoon. It takes time and hard work.

Before we concluded our session, I pointed out that there are usually three steps required of the person who wants to change a behavior: 1) mental assent — he must be willing to replace his faulty thinking with a new belief, 2) conscious choice — he must deliberately choose a new course of action, and 3) deliberate action — he must now act and live in ways that are in keeping with his new beliefs.

The person who puts these steps into practice will discover that his feelings do not automatically change. The first few times this wife undressed in front of her husband, she felt terribly guilty. On more than one occasion she was tempted to revert to her former, more inhibited self. Her faulty reasoning went something like this: "If nakedness is not wrong, why do I still feel guilty?" In counseling, I was able to help her understand that she was dealing with a false guilt, one that was a product of her faulty theology of sex. Repeatedly I told her, "You will not be able to think yourself into right feelings, but if you continue to do the right thing, your emotions will come into line." And they did.

♡ *Love in Action*

Compare your theology of sex with your spouse's. Spend some time discussing them and how they affect your sexual relationship.

♡ *Thought for the Day*

"What is sexually right for us? The answer is learned only in the marriage, by actually practicing sex together with a constant and dear concern for the other's experience and an open expression of one's own. Doing is discovery. Trust allows you both to act before you know. The dependability of your partner allows you to reveal your own deep feelings as you go. A humble hearing allows you to receive your partner's feelings clearly, without threat or misinterpretation. You make your own loving."[5]
— Walter Wangerin, Jr.

♡ *Scripture for the Day*

...may you rejoice in the wife of your youth.... May her breasts satisfy you always, may you ever be captivated by her love.

— Proverbs 5:18,19

♡ *Prayer*

Lord, we thank You for the gift of marriage and the joy of sex within this holy relationship. In Jesus' name we pray. Amen.

chapter 16

What Does a Broken Dishwasher Have to do With Making Love?

*D*on looks up from his computer screen as his secretary hands him a phone message. Glancing at it, he sees that his luncheon appointment has been canceled. On an impulse he telephones his wife, Karen, and invites her to lunch. Excitedly she accepts, and then spends the next twenty minutes trying to find someone to stay with the children. Once that's done, she turns her attention to herself. After a quick shower, she carefully applies make-up and does her hair, all the while thinking about Don. It's been a long time since he's done anything like this. She wants to look her best, wants everything to be perfect.

Glancing at her watch, she realizes that she's late. Rushing out the door, she calls instructions over her shoulder to the baby-sitter. After a hurried drive downtown, she turns into the restaurant parking lot just as Don is getting out of his car. "Perfect," she thinks, giving him her warmest smile.

Although they only have an hour, they make the most of it. And, by the time lunch is over, they are both in a romantic mood. Before going their separate ways, they make plans to devote the entire evening to love. She will feed the children early and get them ready for bed. He will rent a romantic comedy they have both been wanting to see.

Returning to the office, he is in a better mood than he has been in days. His secretary catches him humming the musical theme from "Somewhere in Time." With a knowing smile she comments, "That must have been some lunch."

Alone again, he thinks, "We should do this more often." He makes a mental note to have his secretary put it on his calendar. If a client hadn't canceled lunch today, he would not have had time for Karen. "Thank God," he thinks, "for small favors, and for a wife who is willing to be spontaneous."

Arriving home, Karen finds herself confronted by something of a domestic crisis. The dishwasher has gone on the blink, and the repairman can't come until the day after tomorrow. To make matters worse, the baby-sitter has dirtied every dish in the kitchen. The baby is cranky all afternoon, making it impossible for her to clean up the mess in the kitchen. By five o'clock he is running a fever of 101 degrees, and she is at her wits' end. Whatever romantic feelings she had at lunch have long since fled.

About six o'clock Don walks in with that look in his eye, not to discover the bewitching wife he expected, but an exhausted mother. Being a sensitive husband, he spends the evening helping Karen with the children. "Surely," he reasons, "once we get them in bed we can make up for lost time."

Wrong! Romance is the farthest thing from Karen's mind. Collapsing on the couch, she regales him with a blow by blow account of her dreadful afternoon. He listens with thinly disguised impatience. By now he's ready to promise her anything — a new set of china, the latest super-deluxe dishwasher, a vacation to Hawaii — anything, but to no avail.

Depending on how determined he is, they may still make love, but I can assure you it won't be anything like they had planned.

What happened? That's what most husbands who find themselves in that kind of situation would like to know. What, they wonder, does a broken dishwasher have to do with making love? And most wives, in that situation, end up wondering why they ever married such an insensitive clod.

In truth, she is not overreacting, and he is not an insensitive clod. What we have here is a classic example of the sexual differences between men and women. Hassles that most men would consider minor annoyances can cause a woman to lose all interest in sex, at least for the time being. And, if a couple doesn't understand what's happening, things can rapidly go from bad to worse.

♡♡ *Love in Action*

Recall the last time something like this happened to you. How did you handle it? What will you do differently, if it should happen again?

♡♡ *Thought for the Day*

"A physician named Schwab described the difficulties a woman may experience in playing the three unique roles expected of her; she must be a wife, mistress, and mother. A loving wife who is diligently maintaining her home and caring for the needs of her family is unlikely to feel like a seductive mistress who tempts her husband into the bedroom. Likewise, the requirements of motherhood are at times incompatible with the alternate roles of wife and mistress. Though these 'assignments' seem contradictory, a woman is often asked to switch from one to another on short notice. Her husband can help by getting her away from the wife and mother responsibilities when it is time for her to be his mistress."[1]

— Dr. James Dobson

♡♡ *Scripture for the Day*

There are three things that are too amazing for me, four that I do not understand: the way of an eagle in the sky, the way of a snake on a rock, the way of a ship on the high seas, and the way of a man with a maiden.

— Proverbs 30:18

♡♡ *Prayer*

Lord, help me to remember that when my wife is hurting, sex is probably not what she needs. Teach me to love her in non-sexual ways. In the name of Jesus I pray. Amen.

chapter 17

♡ ♡ ♡ ♡

Paying Bills

*M*ichael is a good teacher, one of the best. His students love him, and he is respected by the administration. He was voted teacher of the year two out of the last three years. Still, he struggles with depression. Not all the time, but at least once a month. Usually right after payday.

Being a creature of habit, he always deposits his paycheck on the day he receives it. After dinner he sits down at the kitchen table and writes out the monthly checks. First he writes his tithe to the church, then he prepares checks for his mortgage payment and utilities, followed by one for his car payment, his life insurance, and his credit card debt. Needless to say, by the time he finishes, there is hardly anything left.

Grimly he stamps the envelopes and places them on the counter to be mailed, before turning in for the night. Tired though he is, sleep won't come. Instead, he tosses and turns, all the while growing more depressed. Though it's pointless, he can't seem to help comparing his meager salary with the big bucks pulled down by his former classmates who went into law or business. By morning, he is determined to leave teaching for greener pastures.

Carol, his wife of eight years, tries to encourage him. "You're doing important work," she says. "You're preparing young people for the future and shaping their characters."

"Big deal!" he says disparagingly. "And for my life-changing work I'm paid a pittance, hardly more than a garbage collector makes. We buy our clothes at Wal-Mart, live in a tiny house, and drive a five-year-old car."

Picking up his battered briefcase he heads for the door, his shoulders slumped. As Carol watches him leave, she is overwhelmed with a feeling of helplessness. She doesn't mind wearing discount store clothes or driving a used car, but she can't seem to make Mike understand. She would do almost anything to free him from his melancholy moods, but for the life of her she is stumped. On an impulse she decides to confide in her mother.

Over lunch she explains the situation in detail, being careful to remind her mother of Mike's good points. "If it wasn't for his monthly bouts with depression," she concludes, "he would be just about the perfect husband."

"Honey," her mother says with a mischievous grin, "when your daddy gets like that, I just take him to the bedroom and make passionate love to him. It makes a new man out of him every time."

Following her mother's advise, Karen begins making love to her husband every time he pays bills. As a result, Mike has stopped talking about leaving teaching, and he is seldom depressed. Oh, by the way, he now pays bills three times a week!

♡♡ *Love in Action*

Be sensitive to your spouse's moods.

If she is tired or depressed, make her a cup of tea. When she shares her troubles, listen, but don't try to fix anything. If she needs some time for herself, volunteer to take care of the children.

If he is tired or depressed, the last thing he wants is a cup of tea, so don't make him one! Instead, take him into the bedroom and make passionate love to him.

♡♡ *Thought for the Day*

"I don't mean to suggest that every problem your husband has can be solved in the bedroom, but I do know that he will be better equipped to deal with the world if he can be assured of your love.... When he feels like a man, he is better able to make manly decisions."[1]

— Richard Exley

♡♡ *Scripture for the Day*

Come, my lover, let us go to the countryside,
let us spend the night in the villages.
...there I will give you my love.

— Song of Songs 7:11,12

♡ *Prayer*

For him:

Lord, help me to remember that when my wife is tired or depressed, the last thing she wants is sex. Make me a compassionate listener even when I don't feel like it. In the name of Jesus I pray. Amen.

For her:

Lord, help me to remember that when my husband is down he needs to be loved. Make me a passionate wife even if I don't feel like it. In the name of Jesus I pray. Amen.

chapter 18

♡ ♡ ♡ ♡

Deep Sharing

*I*n his novel, *Of Mice and Men*, John Steinbeck has a poignant exchange in which a crippled black man laments his loneliness:

"'A guy needs somebody...' Crooks said gently, 'Maybe you can see now. You got George. You know he goin' to come back. S'pose you didn't have nobody. S'pose you couldn't go into the bunk house and play rummy 'cause you was black. How'd you like that? S'pose you had to sit out here an' read books. Sure you could play horseshoes till it got dark, but then you got to read books. Books ain't no good. A guy needs somebody — to be near him.' He whined, 'A guy goes nuts if he ain't got nobody. Don't make no difference who the guy is, long's he's with you. I tell ya,' he cried, 'I tell ya, a guy gets too lonely an' he gets sick.'"[1]

Crooks was right. If a person gets too lonely, he gets sick. But he was sadly mistaken to think that all a person needs is a physical presence. In truth, some of the loneliest people I know are married. For them, loneliness is lying awake in the dead of night, tormented by the regular breathing of their sleeping spouse: If only he had time to hear the cry of her heart, to know her secret fears and share her tentative dreams. If only he could tell her of the aching emptiness he feels deep inside. If only they could really connect — not just physically, but emotionally as well. If only they could be soul mates, sharing their true selves with each other.

What they hunger for is a level of communication which is rare indeed. I call it deep sharing, and it is more than mere talking, more even than what the marriage experts call communication. It is the sharing of your very life. Not just the surface issues either, but the heart and soul of who you truly are — your hidden fears, your secret dreams, the longings too deep for words. Without it, your marriage may be good, but it will never be great.

The Scriptures give us a beautiful picture of the personal transparency inherent in this kind of sharing. When Adam and Eve became man and wife, the Bible says, "The man and his wife were both naked, and they felt no shame."[2] In addition to physical nudity, they were emotionally naked; that is, they had nothing to hide from each other, no secrets. And it was this total transparency that enabled them to truly become one flesh. As C. S. Lewis said, "Eros will have naked bodies; friendships [marriage] naked personalities."[3]

This kind of deep sharing is only possible in an atmosphere of unconditional acceptance. If one of the spouses is judgmental, the other will soon learn to say "right" things rather than "real" things. It will be safer, less confrontational, but it will not be intimate. To be truly intimate, we must share our deepest selves; it is the only way.

♡♡ *Love in Action*

Make a conscious effort to practice unconditional acceptance of the ideas and feelings expressed by your spouse.

♡♡ *Thought for the Day*

"Personal meaning and human value arise only in relationship. Solitude casts doubt on them. Identity, too, is discovered only in relationship. Lacking companions at the level of the soul, I finally cannot find my soul. It always takes another person to show myself to me. Alone, I die."[4]

— Walter Wangerin, Jr.

♡♡ *Scripture for the Day*

The purposes of a man's heart are deep waters, but a man of understanding draws them out.

— Proverbs 20:5

♡♡ *Prayer*

Lord, teach each of us to trust the other with our truest self. In the name of Jesus we pray. Amen.

chapter 19

♡ ♡ ♡ ♡

Keeping Romance in Marriage

*I*t is a wise wife who understands that her husband is not naturally romantic. When he brought her flowers and wrote her poetry during their courtship, he was acting out of character in order to win her love. He does not love her less now that they are married, but neither does he see the importance of continuing his romantic gestures. As far as he is concerned, they were for another time and place.

Though she may well feel slighted, she must not take his lack of romance personally. It is not directed toward her, but is simply a reflection of who he is. If she nags him, he will probably retreat into a stubborn shell. However, if she is patient and imaginative, she can encourage him to become romantic.

Let her make their time together special. Even if dinner is a simple meal, she can serve it by candlelight with mood music. She can invite him to go for a walk or to watch a sunset. Of course, it would be nice if he initiated these romantic gestures, but if he doesn't, she should. In time, he may even learn to take the lead.

Many couples find it helpful to schedule a weekly night out. It is their time together. They may go to dinner, see a movie, take in a concert, or attend a sporting event. What they do is not as important as the fact that they are together, just the two of them. Occasionally, they may "double date," but even then, they make a special effort to pay attention to each other. She holds his hand under the table, he puts his arm around her in the movie; this is their night, and nothing must distract from it.

Other couples have found less traditional ways of keeping romance in their marriage. One caring husband turns down the bed each night and warms his wife's side of the bed so she doesn't have to crawl between cold sheets. A creative wife keeps a journal of special events and reads it each year on their anniversary, providing not only a priceless history of their life together, but also the nostalgic joy of memories relived. Another couple returns to their honeymoon suite each anniversary.

One wife says she will never forget the day her husband came in with a half-a-dozen red roses and said, "Pack your bag. We're leaving in thirty minutes."

Off they went to a quaint little hotel in the Vienna woods about thirty minutes from where they lived. Her husband had previously chosen the hotel, saying he had a very special lady friend he wanted to bring for a weekend getaway. To this day she is convinced the staff didn't think they were married. Her husband's response? "If you're going to have a romantic affair, have it with your mate!"[1]

♡♡ *Love in Action*

Romantic moments seldom just happen. They have to be carefully planned by at least one spouse. With that in mind, begin making plans right now for your next romantic interlude.

♡♡ *Thought for the Day*

"That year of our resurrection Thanne and I spent three days alone at a cabin in Kentucky. It had a tin roof, and the rains came down. In my memory, love sounds like the ceaseless drumming of autumn rains on a metal roof, both light and loud, so loud sometimes we couldn't hear each other; we could only be. And it smells clean. And love has an October bite — the same sharp chill that bit us on county roads in rural Illinois so long ago."[2]

— Walter Wangerin, Jr.

♡♡ *Scripture for the Day*

My lover spoke and said to me, 'Arise, my darling, my beautiful one, and come with me.

See! The winter is past; the rains are over and gone.

Flowers appear on the earth; the season of singing has come, the cooing of doves is heard in our land.

The fig tree forms its early fruit;

the blossoming vines spread their fragrance. Arise, come, my darling; my beautiful one, come with me.

— Song of Songs 2:10-13

♡♡ *Prayer*

Lord, forgive us for allowing the demands of living — job pressures, parenting, financial concerns — to crowd romance out of our marriage. In the name of Jesus we pray. Amen.

chapter 20
♡ ♡ ♡ ♡

Bills, Budgets, and Battles

*N*othing undermines marital harmony faster than trying to decide who's going to manage the family checkbook. When one partner, usually the husband, controls the purse strings, and the other partner, usually the wife, is required to give an account of every penny spent, conflict is inevitable.

"He makes me feel like a child," fumed one young wife who had to have her husband's permission before she could spend a cent. "Who does he think he is, my father?"

Another couple, who had quarreled for years over this very issue, came up with an ingenious solution. Together they adopted a mutually acceptable budget that included an allowance for each of them. Responsibilities were divided between them. He would pay the bills and reconcile the checkbook. She would be responsible for buying groceries and managing the house. Since specific sums were allotted for given categories, she no longer needed his permission to buy groceries or the things necessary to run the house. An added benefit was the allowance. It could be spent any way they wanted and did not have to be accounted for.

Another common source of conflict involves major purchases. When one spouse purchases an appliance, furniture, or a new automobile, without consulting the other, the fur is sure to fly.

This point was driven home to me when I was just a boy and spending the summer with my aunt and uncle. One morning my uncle decided to buy a new ski boat. He invited me to go with him when he went to pick it out. Well do I remember the excitement of choosing a sleek 16-foot outboard with a 75-horsepower Mercury engine. Once we had it outfitted with the required safety equipment, and two pairs of water skis, we pulled it home.

I followed my cousin into the house as he ran to tell his mother the good news. She didn't say anything, but a grim silence settled over the house. She was angry, there was no mistaking that, and for days we all went around as if we were walking on egg shells. No one wanted to become the target of her brooding wrath. Later, we learned that she had wanted to carpet the living room, but had been told by my uncle that they couldn't afford it. Given that information, it is not hard to understand her reaction when, a few days later, he showed up with a brand new boat.

The problem here isn't just money, but respect. When one spouse makes financial decisions without consulting the other, he communicates a clear message. His actions tell her that he doesn't respect her opinion, nor does he care about her feelings.

In order to resolve the misunderstandings about money that are inherent in nearly all marriages, couples must get in touch with the real issue. Her anger is a cry for respect. She wants him to value her opinion, to include her in the decision-making process. His independence is a declaration of his manhood. He wants her to trust him. Once a couple recognizes what is really going on, they can work together to find a mutually acceptable solution.

♡ *Love in Action*

Sit down with your spouse and develop a mutually agreeable plan for managing your money. It should include areas of responsibility, a detailed budget, personal allowances, and guidelines regarding major purchases.

♡ *Thought for the Day*

"Give 10 percent, save 10 percent, and spend the rest with thanksgiving and praise!"[1]

— Charlie W. Shedd

♡♡ *Scripture for the Day*

Command them to do good, to be rich in good deeds, and to be generous and willing to share. In this way they will lay up treasure for themselves as a firm foundation for the coming age, so that they may take hold of the life that is truly life.

— 1 Timothy 6:18,19

♡♡ *Prayer*

Lord, teach us to see material possessions as a blessing to be enjoyed and shared. In the name of Jesus we pray. Amen.

chapter 21

A Different Shade of Purple

As the plane taxis toward the gate, I realize that I am bone weary. It is Saturday afternoon, and for the past week I have been on a whirlwind book tour. My body aches from too many flights and too little exercise. I am stressed out, but there is no relief in sight. In my office a week's worth of mail and phone messages await me, and I haven't even started on Sunday's sermon. Although I hunger for Brenda's home cooking and the comfort of my own bed, that will have to wait.

Brenda meets me at the baggage carrousel, and we drive to the church after claiming my luggage. While going through my mail, I discover that my publisher has sent me a copy of the four-color brochure promoting my newest book. Looking at it, I experience a feeling of accomplishment, even importance.

Hastily I sort the rest of my mail, and in a matter of minutes my desk is clear. Stuffing my phone messages into my briefcase, I switch off the lights and head for the door.

Once we are in the car, I hand the brochure to Brenda and turn toward home.

Taking one look at it, she says, "They didn't get the color right. It should be a different shade of purple."

A flash of white hot anger seizes me. This isn't about color. Besides, it's too late to do anything about it now. The brochure has already been mailed out. Why, I fume, can't Brenda ever see the big picture instead of getting hung up on the details?

Slamming on the brakes, I skid to a stop. Angrily I jerk the brochure out of her hand and wad it up.

Opening my door, I fling it into the street. "If it's that bad," I say through clinched teeth, "let's throw the stupid thing out."

Although she is stunned by my sudden fury, Brenda says nothing, and anger hangs heavily in the silence between us.

After several miles, the heat of my anger begins to wane; still, I cannot bring myself to apologize. Instead, I rehearse my self-justifying arguments in my mind. "Yes, I overreacted, but I'm not myself. I'm stressed out."

A saner part of me rejects such rationalization. Even as the strength of a product is determined by its breaking point, so a person's character is revealed in times of stress.

Looking inward, I am forced to admit that I was angry because Brenda did not feed my ego. When she saw the brochure, I expected her to be impressed — not with the brochure necessarily, but with me! I wanted her to tell me how proud she was to be married to a man God was using in such an important way. Instead, she criticized the color, and I felt attacked.

Turning into our driveway, I push the button on the garage door opener and wait impatiently for the door to go up. After driving into the garage, I switch off the car engine, and we sit in gloomy silence for what seems like several minutes.

Finally Brenda speaks. "I didn't mean to make you mad. I had no idea you would take my remarks personally."

"You always do that," I respond, still smarting with anger. "Anytime I show you anything, you only see the imperfections. You never say, 'That's great,' or, 'I'm so happy for you.' It's always, 'The color is not quite right,' or 'The lettering is wrong.'"

For awhile she sits in thoughtful silence before finally saying, "I want to change, I really do, but you will have to help me."

"How can I help you?" I ask impatiently. "It's your problem, not mine."

Ignoring my sarcasm, she continues, "I'm a perfectionist. It's a family trait, one that I inherited from my father. When I look at anything, my eye is naturally drawn to the slightest imperfection. In the future try asking me what I like best. That will help me focus on what I like, rather than the imperfections."

Conflicting emotions struggle inside me. I am touched by Brenda's vulnerability, but I am still angry. Her request for help appeals to the hero in me. I want to mount my white charger and ride to the rescue, but to do so I will have to let go of my anger.

At last I reach across the car and take her hand. "I'm sorry," I say. "There is absolutely no excuse for the way I acted."

That painful incident occurred nearly ten years ago, and I am thankful to report that we are doing much better. With my help Brenda is responding more positively. And if she does revert to her perfectionism, I try not to take it personally. As a consequence, I am less inclined to react in anger.

♡♡ *Love in Action*

If you have any habits or characteristics that repeatedly create conflict in your marriage, ask your mate to help you change. List some specific things he/she can do to help.

♡♡ *Thought for the Day*

"It is not easy for us to change. But it is possible. And it is our glory as human beings."[1]

— M. Scott Peck, M.D.

❧ Scripture for the Day

The wisdom of the prudent is to give thought to their ways, but the folly of fools is deception.

— Proverbs 14:8

❧ Prayer

Lord, I confess that change isn't easy for me. When my mate suggests it, I become defensive, even argumentative. Forgive me and help me to be willing to change. In the name of Jesus I pray. Amen.

chapter 22

♡ ♡ ♡ ♡

Help, I'm Angry!

"*T*he state of marriage," according to David Mace, world-renowned marriage and family counselor, "generates in normal people more anger than they are likely to experience in any other type of relationship in which they habitually find themselves."[1]

If he's right, and I believe he is, then we need to ask ourselves why. Why does marriage, which is potentially the most intimate of all relationships, generate so much anger? Remember, Mace is not talking about dysfunctional marriages. If he were, his statement would be self-explanatory. It is no mystery why a betrayed spouse feels angry, or why the wife of an alcoholic finds herself in a rage. No, the question before us is, "Why does a relatively good marriage generate so much anger?"

It must be because we care more about our marriage than we do about any other relationship in our life. We care what other people do, but only up to a point. Because they are not a permanent part of our life, their actions have no lasting effect upon us, and we seldom allow them to make us angry for more than a brief moment. In marriage, things are different. What our spouse does, what he/she feels, or thinks, has a direct bearing upon our own well-being.

Although love and anger are poles apart, they are not opposite emotions; rather, they are two sides of the same coin. Love is the positive expression of the deep feelings we have for our spouse, while anger is the negative expression of those very same feelings. It is accurate, I believe, to say that the amount of anger we are capable of feeling is often in direct proportion to how much we love.

Having said that, let me hasten to add that the inappropriate expression of anger is one of the most destructive forces in a relationship. Mismanaged, it can tear a marriage apart. No matter how much we love our spouse, it is virtually impossible to overcome the hurt and distrust caused by our reckless anger.

As one emotionally devastated wife so aptly put it: "It takes a hundred kind words to undo the damage from a single angry word."

It is critically important, therefore, to manage the anger in a relationship. Find nondestructive ways of dealing with it. Make it a friend instead of a foe. Learn to make it productive.

According to Howard and Charlotte Clinebell, authors of *The Intimate Marriage*, "Occasional outbursts may make it possible for the marriage partners to be more caring and compassionate at other times. A relationship strong enough to take such outbursts in its stride is a healthy one. Providing a place where one can safely drain off hostility that has accumulated in the outside world is one of the important mental health functions of a good marriage."[2]

They go on to point out, "Chronic verbal attacking is not a means of maintaining a healthy marriage."[3] Remember, anger is a powerful emotion and should be handled with care.

♡ *Love in Action*

Take some time with your spouse and discuss the role anger plays in your marriage. Is it constructive or destructive? How could it be better handled?

♡ *Thought for the Day*

"We not only need to know how to deal with our anger in different ways at different times but also how most appropriately to match the right time with the right style of expression."[4]

— M. Scott Peck, M.D.

♡ *Scripture for the Day*

Reckless words pierce like a sword, but the tongue of the wise brings healing.

— Proverbs 12:18

♡ *Prayer*

Forgive me, Lord, for I have sinned in my anger. Heal the wounds my reckless words have caused and set a watch over my lips. Let no angry word come from my mouth. In the name of Jesus I pray. Amen.

chapter 23

♡♡♡♡

Stick to the Issue

*I*t has been an exhausting seven weeks, and only now that the project is finished does Bob realize how tired he really is. The constant pressure, the long hours, and the ever-present deadlines have taken their toll. He would like nothing better than some time to himself, preferably a few hours on the golf course.

Unfortunately, that will have to wait. This weekend he needs to catch up on all the household responsibilities that have fallen by the way while he concentrated on his big project at work.

Sensing his weariness, his wife Ann says, "I want you to take tomorrow for yourself. Sleep in if you feel like it. Spend the afternoon golfing. Just get away and take some time for yourself. You've earned it."

"Thanks, honey," Bob replies, "but I can't. The lawn has got to be mowed. Both of the cars need to be serviced, and if I don't get the bills paid we're going to have creditors knocking on our door."

But Ann insists, and early Saturday morning Bob sets off for the golf course. Later he joins his friend Kent for an early lunch before heading for the local university football game. All in all it turns out to be a totally relaxing day.

Ann's day is anything but relaxing. After cleaning the house while doing several loads of laundry, she finally makes it to the supermarket. Returning home, she puts the groceries away, bathes the children, and prepares dinner. She is tired, but it is a good tiredness. It has been a productive day.

Bob is whistling as he steps through the front door a few minutes later, causing Ann to smile to herself. "It's nice to see him relaxed," she thinks. Returning his cheery greeting, she goes to the kitchen to finish dinner, while he heads for his favorite recliner in the den. Along the way he deposits his golf clubs in the living room and tosses his jacket over a chair.

Soon he is engrossed in the sports section and returns to reality only when Ann calls him to dinner. Hoisting himself out of the recliner, he leaves the newspaper where it falls. Never mind that the magazine holder is at his elbow. Bowing his head while their youngest recites the blessing, he takes time to be thankful before digging in. Ann has prepared spaghetti with his favorite meat sauce, and he wolfs it down without so much as a peep of praise. Burping with satisfaction, he adjourns to the couch to channel surf until bedtime.

While he relaxes in front of the television, Ann methodically clears the table. As she is putting the last of the dishes into the dishwasher, he calls from the family room. "Honey, could you bring me a Coke? And while you're at it, how about fixing me a bag of microwave popcorn?"

Shortly thereafter he falls asleep on the couch. When he awakens, the house is quiet. Shutting off the television, he heads upstairs. Pausing at the bedroom door, he watches Ann turn down the bed with an unnecessary vigor. Sensing her mood, he asks, "What's wrong?"

"Nothing!" she snaps.

A wiser man would have turned out the light and gone to sleep, hoping things would improve by morning. Not Bob.

"What do you mean nothing?" he demands. "You're about to burst an artery. Your blood pressure must be at least 190 over 130."

"What concern is that of yours?" Ann parries, crawling into bed. Deliberately she turns on her side facing the wall.

"While you're out frolicking with your buddies," she says accusingly, "I'm cleaning your house, doing your laundry, looking after your children, and cooking your dinner."

"Wait a minute," Bob protests, holding up his hands. "It was your idea for me to take the day off."

"Yes, it was," Ann acknowledges, "and I'm glad you did. I don't begrudge you a few hours to yourself. What makes me mad is the way you destroy the house, especially after I've worked so hard cleaning it."

"What are you talking about?" Bob asks in amazement.

"You know good and well what I'm talking about," Ann retorts. "The house was perfectly straight when you got home, and now look at it. Your golf clubs are in the living room, as is your jacket. The den is an absolute wreck. You've got newspapers scattered everywhere. Your empty Coke can is on the end table, and the couch is covered with popcorn kernels."

What can he say? Though he has not seen it until that very minute, the messy evidence is overwhelming. In short order he has nullified Ann's best efforts. Rather than apologizing, he leaps to his feet and grabs her by the hand. Leading her across the hall, he kicks open the door to her craft room.

"Don't talk to me about cluttering up the house," he says, "until you do something about this mess. Look at it. It's worse than a pig sty."

Now it's her turn, and she marches him downstairs and into the garage. "How dare you talk to me about my craft room," she says, "when the garage looks like this."

How long Bob and Ann continue this foolishness depends on their energy level and temperaments. Whether they run down quickly, or carry on for most of the night, it is sure that nothing will be resolved. Until they learn to stick to the issue, their marital conflicts will remain destructive rather than productive.

♡ Love in Action

Did you catch a glimpse of yourself in this story? Do you and your spouse have the same fights again and again because you won't stick to the issue? If so, honestly acknowledge your behavior to God and to your spouse. Now make a commitment to change. With God's help you can.

♡ Thought for the Day

"Effective conflict-resolution communication focuses on issues rather than attacking personalities. This is the chief characteristic of productive, as distinguished from futile, arguments."[1]

— Howard and Charlotte Clinebell

♡ Scripture for the Day

...encourage one another and build each other up.... Live in peace with each other.... Make sure that nobody pays back wrong for wrong, but always try to be kind to each other and to everyone else.

— 1 Thessalonians 5:11,13,15

♡ Prayer

Lord, teach us how to be kind; how to live at peace, especially with each other. In the name of Jesus we pray. Amen.

chapter 24

♡ ♡ ♡

Making Anger Productive

*M*arital quarrels are inevitable, and every couple will disagree sooner or later, even committed Christians. While conflict is uncomfortable, it is not necessarily bad. If quarrels can be used to resolve differences, then anger can be constructive, rather than destructive. With that thought in mind, let me offer five rules for making anger productive.

Rule # 1: Don't attack your spouse. Use "I" messages rather than "you" messages. An "I" message focuses on the speaker rather than the person being spoken to. For example, "You make me so mad" is a "you" message, and it attacks the person being addressed. On the other hand, "I am feeling angry" is an "I" message, and it focuses on the speaker, making him responsible for his feelings. By using "I" messages, you give your spouse a chance to evaluate what you are saying, without feeling the need to defend himself or herself.

Rule # 2: Practice reflective listening. Reflective listening is demanding under the best of conditions, and it can seem almost impossible in the heat of an argument. But if you can force yourself to listen carefully before you speak, you will discover that the rewards are well worth the effort.

In the heat of an argument we are almost always tempted to defend ourselves, or at least to explain ourselves. Reflective listening encourages us to control that defensive instinct. Instead of defending yourself, you might say: "It sounds like you feel hurt and angry when I make a major decision without consulting you."

A statement like that does at least two things. First, it lets your spouse know that you hear what he/she is saying and that his/her thoughts and feelings are important. Second, it allows him/her to clarify and expand until you truly understand why he/she feels the way he/she does. Practice reflective listening consistently, and you will not only grow in your understanding of each other, but you will resolve some thorny issues as well.

Rule # 3: Stick to the issue! Many couples never resolve anything when they fight, because they can't stick to the issue. As soon as one of them starts to "win," the other one changes the subject and mounts an attack.

H. Norman Wright, in *Communication: Key to Your Marriage*, writes, "There is an old story about a sheepherder in Wyoming who would observe the behavior of wild animals during the winter. Packs of wolves, for example, would sweep into the valley and attack the bands of wild horses. The horses would form a circle with their heads at the center of the circle and kick out at the wolves, driving them away. Then the sheepherder saw the wolves attack a band of wild jackasses. The animals also formed a circle, but they formed it with their heads out toward the wolves. When they began to kick, they ended up kicking one another."[1]

The moral of this story should be readily obvious. When you and your spouse quarrel, you can be as wise as wild horses or as dumb as wild jackasses. You can kick the problem, or you can kick one another.

Rule # 4: Don't hit below the belt. If you have been married for any length of time, you know where your spouse is vulnerable, and vice versa; you know how to hurt each other.

I'm thinking of a man whose first wife left him for another man. When he asked her to come back, she laughed and ridiculed him. When he demanded an explanation, she said, "You're a lousy lover. You've never once satisfied me." Of course, he was devastated.

A couple of years passed and he remarried. During a tender moment he shared that painful incident with his new wife. She responded with affection and affirmation. However, some months later, in the heat of battle, she threw it in his face. "No wonder," she said cruelly, "your first wife took a lover."

She won the argument, but it was a long time before her husband ever trusted her again.

Rule # 5: Don't go to bed angry. Nothing is more important than ending the conflict and renewing the relationship before calling it a day. Unresolved anger can turn into bitterness almost overnight. That's why Paul said, "...Do not let the sun go down while you are still angry, and do not give the devil a foothold."[2]

♡ *Love in Action*

Memorize the five steps to productive conflict resolution. Make a covenant with your spouse that you will always "fight fairly." Then seal that covenant by committing it to God in prayer.

♡ *Thought for the Day*

"If someone hurts you, first try to figure out whether that hurt was intentional or not. Not every hurt is an attack."

— John Maxwell

♡ *Scripture for the Day*

...Everyone should be quick to listen, slow to speak and slow to become angry, for man's anger does not bring about the righteous life that God desires.

— James 1:19,20

♡♡ *Prayer*

Lord, empower us to resolve our marital conflicts in ways that are constructive rather than destructive. In the name of Jesus we pray. Amen.

chapter 25

Making a House a Home

$\mathcal{S}$ ome time ago, Brenda and I took an afternoon and visited some new homes. The floor plans were creative, the furnishings expensively tasteful, and the color schemes carefully coordinated. As we toured these "dream" homes I could not help wondering if these houses would ever really become homes.

A home is more than just a house with people living in it. It is a place where love and laughter reside, a place where family memories are made, a place where children are loved and cared for. A home doesn't just happen. It doesn't evolve simply because a man and woman marry and bear children. It takes time, love, and commitment to turn a house into a home.

In my childhood family, Dad and Mom were equally responsible for making our house a home. Dad was clearly the head of the house. Without being dictatorial or overbearing, he provided the spiritual leadership that gave our family its purpose. Mom set the emotional tone. With a special grace she managed to create a house of love, a home where we were nurtured, both emotionally and spiritually.

At the very center of everything my parents did was an unconditional commitment to the Lord Jesus Christ. Early in their marriage, they made a choice to follow the Lord. Like Joshua of old, my father determined, "...as for me and my household, we will serve the Lord."[1]

The sound of Dad's prayers, like his faith, filled our house and our lives. Well do I recall awaking in the pre-dawn darkness to the sound of his voice raised in prayer. Distinctly, I can remember throwing the covers back and tiptoeing down the hall to stand just outside the door to the living room. Never have I felt more loved, more secure, than when I heard Dad call my name to our Heavenly Father in prayer.

Nor can I ever forget the afternoons when I passed Mother's bedroom door, opened just a crack so she could listen for the little ones, and saw her on her knees beside her bed with the Scriptures open before her. It's faith and commitment like that which makes a house a home!

My parents' commitment to God and His Church gave our family structure and stability. On Saturday afternoons we polished our shoes and took baths in preparation for Sunday. Saturday evenings we gathered around the kitchen table to study our Sunday school lessons and recite our memory verses. These shared times bonded us for life, made us a family, and turned our house into a home.

♡ *Love in Action*

Think of the things you and your mate are doing to make your house a home. Now make a list of some additional things you can do and immediately begin putting them into practice.

♡ *Thought for the Day*

"My father was not a man much given to words. I can't remember a single time when he sat me down and imparted to me a moral axiom or a spiritual principle. Yet almost everything I know about life and godliness I learned from him — not so much from what he said, but from how he lived."

— Richard Exley

♡ *Scripture for the Day*

"Now fear the LORD and serve him with all faithfulness. Throw away the gods your forefathers worshipped beyond the River and in Egypt, and serve the LORD. But if serving the LORD seems undesirable to you, then choose for yourselves this day whom you will serve, whether the gods your forefathers served beyond the River, or the gods of the Amorites, in whose land you are living. But as for me and my household, we will serve the LORD."

— Joshua 24:14,15

♡♡ *Prayer*

Lord, we choose to serve You. With Your help we will rear our children in the fear and admonition of the Lord. In Your Holy name we pray. Amen.

chapter 26

♡ ♡ ♡ ♡

The Birth of the First Child

She loves her three-month-old baby, but she's exhausted.

She loves her job, but she's exhausted.

She loves her husband, friends, parents, walking in the park, reading, gourmet cooking, and having twenty minutes a week to herself. But she's exhausted. She's having a predictable marriage crisis — the birth of her first child.

It isn't supposed to be like this, at least not according to her way of thinking. She is not supposed to have moments when she resents her baby, her husband, everything. What happened to her idyllic vision of motherhood? You know, the one in which a young, model-perfect mom sings lullabies to her contented baby as she rocks him to sleep, while outside huge snowflakes drift down, creating a winter wonderland. Later, she will tuck him in his perfect baby bed before joining her husband in front of the fireplace for a quiet talk and some tender loving care.

But it is not at all like that for her. She has never been so exhausted in all her life. Her nights are a marathon of feedings and diapers and tiny, insufficient snatches of sleep. During the day she functions by rote, zombie-like, trying to maintain all of her pre-baby responsibilities, plus give her undivided attention to this little creature, who resembles nothing so much as a bottomless pit of needs. Somehow she manages, after a sort, though she cannot imagine how.

She is having a predictable marriage crisis — the birth of her first baby.

Her husband is experiencing a crisis of his own. Like his wife, he is thrilled and thankful for their baby, but nothing in the birthing classes prepared him for the drastic changes that have occurred in his life. His wife seems totally preoccupied with the baby. She never has time or energy for him, at least that's the way it seems. They never do anything together any more. And, as crazy as it sounds, he almost feels jealous of his own child.

He's having a predictable marriage crisis — the birth of their first child.

"So," you may be wondering, "how do we prepare for the birth of our first child? And once he or she has arrived, what can we do to minimize the stress while enhancing our joy?"

Begin by being aware of what's happening. There is nothing wrong with you. Most new parents have a wide range of emotional reactions, especially the first few months. They feel absolutely euphoric joy and, in turn, unbelievable resentment. They also have moments when they feel overwhelmed by the awesome responsibilities of parenting.

It also helps to realize that the initial draining schedule of a newborn does not last forever. Things will get better. See the child for who he is, a person in his own right. He is not a sexual rival nor a substitute for either spouse.

Finally, develop flexibility in meeting your spouse's needs. Expanding the ability to express frustrations, feelings, and even delaying some need-satisfaction will be a major step toward restoring marital understanding and closeness.

♡ *Love in Action*

If you have just had your first child, use this material as a basis for discussing what's happening in your relationship. Honestly share your feelings. Even if you can't change anything, talking about it often relieves stress, even as it enables you to reconnect with your spouse.

♡ *Thought for the Day*

"We spend many years preparing for our vocation and in some instances work into it gradually. We spend six months to four years becoming acquainted with our spouse prior to marriage and this relationship gradually grows and develops. Not so with parenthood! We are aware that the child is coming, and then abruptly — a minute later — this new stranger is alive, loud and demanding." [1]

— H. Norman Wright

❥ Scripture for the Day

May your father and mother be glad; may she who gave you birth rejoice!

— Proverbs 23:25

❥ Prayer

Lord, we dedicate our son/daughter to You. We pray that You will protect him/her from accident and injury. Take sickness and disease from him/her. Give him/her a heart that hungers and thirsts for righteousness, eyes that look with compassion upon the needy, hands that touch and heal, and a desire to ever do Your eternal will. Fulfill Your purposes in his/her life. In Jesus' name we pray. Amen.

chapter 27
♡ ♡ ♡ ♡

Help, I'm a Father!

*W*ell do I remember the joy radiating from Ron and Charlene's faces when I visited them in the hospital a few hours after their first child was born. In spite of the fact that the delivery had been difficult, they were still awed by it all. For them, the miracle of birth was a deeply spiritual experience, one that left them profoundly moved. With parental pride they presented their newborn daughter for my inspection. Ron took out his camera and insisted that I allow him to photograph me holding the baby.

Equally well do I remember Ron's telephone call a week or so after they took the baby home. He was at his wits' end. Sleeplessness and stress had rubbed his emotions raw. Tearfully he confessed, "Pastor, this is not at all what I expected. All this baby does is eat and sleep and poop. And cry! Boy can she cry!"

Hesitantly he continued, shame making his voice almost inaudible, "I don't think I love her. I almost wish she wasn't here."

He paused then, waiting, I think, for my rebuke. Instead, I shared the details of Brenda's struggle to accept Leah. Leah's birth had also been difficult, leaving Brenda exhausted and riddled with pain. Then she suffered a major hemorrhage and had to have emergency surgery to save her life. During her recovery she had little or no desire to see or hold her baby. Later she told me that she couldn't help blaming Leah for everything that had happened to her. Of course, her feelings passed, and her love for Leah is now something to behold.

After hearing me out, Ron felt better. Just knowing that he wasn't the only parent who had such feelings helped, but the clincher was the relationship Brenda and Leah now share. Their closeness is obvious to all. Their relationship goes beyond the normal mother/daughter thing. They are also best friends. By the time we said good-bye, Ron had every confidence that his negative feelings would pass, to be replaced by the love of a father for his daughter.

And they did. Today, Ron not only shares a very special relationship with his firstborn, but he is also the proud father of four additional children — two sons and two more lovely daughters!

♡ Love in Action

If you are preparing for the birth of your first child, talk with some friends who have already had a baby. Ask them what to expect. Seek their advice regarding the adjustments you will likely have to make.

♡ Thought for the Day

"...family study experts say that the birth of the first child is a major crisis for many couples....Most couples have only a vague idea of what is entailed in the task of parenthood let alone the changes which occur in the marital relationship. One of the biggest adjustments is how to integrate this new person into the family so all three lives are enhanced."[1]

— H. Norman Wright

♡ Scripture for the Day

Sons [and daughters] are a heritage from the LORD, children a reward from him. Like arrows in the hands of a warrior are sons [and daughters] born in one's youth. Blessed is the man whose quiver is full of them....

— Psalm 127:3-5

♡ Prayer

Lord, we thank You for the gift of children. Empower us to be the kind of parents needed to rear godly children. In Your Holy name we pray. Amen.

chapter 28

When Illness Strikes

*I*t started with a low-grade fever, followed by vomiting which lasted for a couple of days. Since Leah, who was only eight months old, appeared to be dehydrating, we decided to take her to a pediatrician. After examining her, the doctor gave her an injection. Instantly her tiny body grew rigid, her eyes rolled back in her head, and her limbs jerked spastically.

Quickly the doctor ordered a second injection, but to no avail. Then a third, which also proved futile. Scooping Leah's rigid body into his arms, he ran for his car, shouting for his nurse to drive. Brenda hurried after them, and in seconds they were racing for the hospital.

I followed in my own car, fear pushing me to the point of panic. All I could see was Leah's tiny body rigid and spastic, her face contorted. Would I ever see her smile again, or hear her giggle contentedly as Brenda pinned a dry diaper on her freshly powered bottom?

Terrifying thoughts of her death gripped my mind. With a Herculean effort I dismissed them, only to have them return a minute later. There were other thoughts too, almost as terrifying — Leah, brain-damaged or growing up afflicted with epilepsy.

Skidding to a stop in the hospital parking lot, I rushed after the doctor who was disappearing through the emergency entrance. For the next two and one-half hours the doctors worked to save Leah's life, leaving Brenda and me alone to await the outcome.

In desperation I called our families, begging them to pray. As I hung up the phone, a feeling of desolation washed over me. Standing beside the now silent phone, at the end of the empty hallway, I felt terribly alone.

After getting hold of myself, I made my way back to Brenda, who was nervously pacing the floor just outside the emergency area. We clung to each other and cried and prayed. Never had life seemed so empty of hope, so crowded with pain and fear. Together we faced the unthinkable — Leah might not live, and if she did she might never be the same again. Yet even as we came to grips with the terrifying possibility of Leah's death, we also began to sense God's presence.

The possibility of Leah's death was not diminished, it was no less real. Yet in a way that I cannot explain, we were suddenly at peace. Our hearts and minds were filled with the assurance that no matter what happened, whether Leah lived or died, God's grace would be sufficient. Somehow life would still be worth living.

Finally the doctor emerged, looking exhausted but relieved. Leah was out of danger; she would live. The medical staff wanted to keep her in the hospital for a few more days. There were a number of tests they needed to do. He listened patiently as we bombarded him with a barrage of questions. After answering as best he could, he excused himself, and we were left alone once again.

Only we weren't alone — God was with us! We were relieved, yet not nearly to the extent that might be expected. The real relief had already come — the peace of God that passes all understanding.

♡ *Love in Action*

Make a commitment to each other and God to daily practice the spiritual disciplines of the Word of God and prayer. Do this and you will be prepared when life's crises come.

♡ *Thought for the Day*

"*In one sense, the peace of God that Elaine St. Johns experienced was the result of His sovereign grace. Suddenly, instantly, she possessed it — or more likely, it possessed her. She didn't do anything to generate it. It was just there!*

"*Yet in a deeper and more profound sense, it was the consequence of her spiritual disciplines. For some time she had been preparing for this moment, or one like it. Daily she been hiding the Word in her heart, had been tuning her ear for God's voice. 'Then,' to use her words, 'in a moment of extremity, when*

I could do nothing of myself, when I had no time to labor, or pray, or even think, the fruitage appeared as instant grace — "Lo, I am with you always."" [1]

— Richard Exley

♡ *Scripture for the Day*

"I have told you these things, so that in me you may have peace. In this world you will have trouble. But take heart! I have overcome the world."

— John 16:33

♡ *Prayer*

Lord, teach us to come to You often during the peaceful days of our lives, that we may know where to find You in the dark midnight hour. In Jesus' name we pray. Amen.

chapter 29

♡ ♡ ♡ ♡

Overcoming Adversity

*I*llness of any kind, especially a critical illness, produces stress. If the critically ill patient is a child, the stress is magnified many times over. In fact, research indicates that many marriages fail under the pressure. In addition to the obvious difficulties of maintaining anything resembling a normal home and lifestyle, there are also enormous psychological pressures — pressures that husbands and wives react to in decidedly different ways.

For John, the overriding feeling is a sense of helplessness. His three-year-old son is desperately ill, fighting for his life, and John is powerless to save him. He is used to taking charge and getting things done, but this is a situation in which nothing he does makes any difference. Like many assertive men, he responds with anger.

At first he takes out his exasperation on the doctors and other health professionals, accusing them of incompetence or worse. As his son slides ever closer to death, he turns his anger on members of his own family as well, especially his wife.

His rage is really directed toward the disease that threatens his precious child, or toward God, Who has "let" this happen, or even toward his own helplessness. But not knowing how to deal with it, he takes it out on those closest to him.

If John's temperament were less assertive, he might simply "escape." He might lose himself in his work, or in taking care of the household chores and the other children. Men who respond in this way frequently deny the seriousness of the situation, refusing to face the possibility of their child's impending death. This effectively isolates them from both their spouse and their sick child. While there is little overt hostility in this response, the damage to the marriage is no less.

Susan, John's wife, has no time for anger. Instead, she totally invests herself in her sick child at the expense of John and the other children. For her, there is no world outside of that small hospital room, no concern except the welfare of her suffering son. When other concerns press upon her, she rationalizes: "Others will have to understand. This is an emergency, nothing else matters right now." The resulting jealousies and tensions only add to the family trauma.

Complicating everything is the inevitable conflict over marital intimacy.

Susan loses all interest, while John's sexual desires continue unabated. To her way of thinking, he is disgusting. "How?" she asks me, "can he even think of sex at a time like this?"

John is no less judgmental. As far as he is concerned, Susan has an unhealthy fixation on their sick child.

John and Susan's only hope is to realize that each is coping with the crisis in the way most natural to him or her. John desires sexual intimacy with his wife, not because he is an unfeeling brute, as she supposes, but because it is the only way he can cope with his pain and the impending loss of his son.

Nor does Susan have an abnormal fixation on her sick child, as her husband accuses. She does not love John any less, she has not forgotten the other children or the family's needs. It is just that right now her child is critically ill, and all of her maternal instincts demand that she rush to his defense. The fact that she can do nothing but maintain her bedside vigil does not, in any way, diminish her sense of responsibility. She does not explain her feelings, doesn't even imagine that she should. Doesn't her husband feel the same way? Isn't this his child too?

If John and Susan will accept the legitimacy of each other's feelings, they can move beyond resentment to support. They can then face the common enemy (illness) united, arm-in-arm, rather than mistakenly attacking each other.

Such mutual support is absolutely mandatory if a marriage is to survive the serious illness, or death, of a child.

♡ *Love in Action*

Discuss the different ways men and women respond to the same situation. Identify some specific ways you and your spouse respond differently to a given set of circumstances. Make a commitment to accept each other's feelings rather than judging them.

♡ *Thought for the Day*

"The person I loved but couldn't seem to communicate with was still very much in my thoughts, my prayers, my heart. But I didn't know how to respond, what I should say or do, or if even I should say or do anything. There was a specific, unresolved conflict that I didn't know how to handle. I had gotten advice from others, but the advice was conflicting, and I still was confused. Should I be firm and unyielding, make the person pay the consequences? Or should I be forgiving and pay them myself?

"I decided to respond with warmth and forgiveness."[1]

— Ken Gire

♡ *Scripture for the Day*

Praise be to the God and Father of our Lord Jesus Christ, the Father of compassion and the God of all comfort, who comforts us in all our troubles, so that we can comfort those in any trouble with the comfort we ourselves have received from God.

— 2 Corinthians 1:3,4

♡♡ *Prayer*

Lord, teach us to comfort each other when life's inevitable crises come. In the name of Jesus we pray. Amen.

chapter 30

The Day We Kidnapped Dad

*P*aula's husband is the pastor of a large congregation, and the demands of ministry are continually encroaching on their family time. Try as she may, she cannot convince him to take his day off. Always there is an important meeting or an emergency of some kind. Though he promises to reschedule their family time, he seldom does.

Finally, Paula decides to take matters into her own hands. On a Wednesday afternoon, just before school is to be dismissed, she stops by his office at the church. "Honey," she asks sweetly, "how about riding with me to pick up the children from school?"

"Sorry," Bo replies, "I have an appointment in ten minutes."

"It's been rescheduled. I checked with your secretary on the way in."

"Well, in that case, let's go."

Once the children are in the car, Paula says, "Let's do something really wild and crazy."

Giving her a sharp glance, Bo asks, "Like what?"

"Instead of going back to the church, let's drive to the coast and stay in a condo for a couple of days. The kids can play on the beach, and we can spend some quality time together."

Always the practical man, Bo replies, "That's a terrific idea, only it won't work. I'm scheduled to preach in less than four hours. Besides, my calendar is really full for the next few days."

By now the kids are clamoring to go. "Please, Daddy," they beg. "Oh, pretty please."

Without further discussion, Paula turns on the highway and heads for the coast. "Be serious, sweetheart," Bo coaxes. "I can't just skip out on the church."

With a mischievous look, Paula says, "It is all taken care of. Your associate will preach tonight, and your secretary has rescheduled all of your appointments."

"What about clothes?" Bo asks meekly. "And toiletries?"

"Everything's in the trunk. All you have to do is sit back and relax."

Needless to say, that getaway became the highlight of their year. The children still talk about the time they kidnapped Dad and had him all to themselves for three full days.

Most couples probably don't have that kind of flexibility, but even the most confining schedule can be made to accommodate some creativity. Maybe all your busy spouse needs is someone who will take charge and plan some real time together. The next time you are tempted to complain that you never have any time together, do something creative instead.

♡ *Love in Action*

Examine your calendar for the last ninety days. Have you been giving your family priority on your days off? List some of the things you have done together. Discuss positive ways to improve your family time.

♡ *Thought for the Day*

"We also started the tradition of going off alone together. We began to realize we needed extended times alone together —more than just a morning. So we began to look for opportunities to plan just-for-two getaways. We couldn't afford to hire a sitter to come and stay with our children for an extended time, and our parents lived too far away. But we did have friends —very good friends — who offered to keep our three Indians. We reciprocated by keeping their two girls, and we're sure we got the better deal!"[1]

— Dave and Claudia Arp

♡ *Scripture for the Day*

If a man has recently married, he must not be sent to war or have any other duty laid on him. For one year he is to be free to stay at home and bring happiness to the wife he has married.

— Deuteronomy 24:5

♡♡ *Prayer*

Lord, teach us to be creative instead of complaining. Help us to truly connect with each other and our children. In the name of Jesus we pray. Amen.

chapter 31

Making Family Traditions

*A*bout twenty years ago my wife's parents and two other couples jointly purchased a small ranch in East Texas in preparation for their retirement. In the early days, when retirement was still ten years away, they each built a one-room cabin to use on weekends and holidays. After their retirement these cabins would grow into wonderfully rustic three-bedroom homes.

They called their ranch "Vallew." They arrived at the name by combining the first initials from their last names. "v" is from Vorse, "E" is from Easter, and "w" is from Wallace. The "A-L-L" is for all of them. The name itself symbolizes the deep feelings they have for each other and the dreams they share of enjoying their friendship as long as they live. That may seem corny to some, but I find it touching, especially in light of the throwaway relationships so characteristic of our age.

It wasn't long until Vallew became a getaway place for Brenda and me. Some of our daughter Leah's favorite memories were made there. There was the time we spent a week at the ranch with my brother and his family. For two days Don and I worked like slaves building the kids an elaborate tree house. In the evenings we took turns riding a mean-spirited old pony named Shorty. Afterwards we told childhood stories in front of the Franklin stove, while feasting on chili and Polish sausages cooked over a campfire. All in all we had the time of our lives.

Thanksgiving at Vallew soon became a family tradition. Joining us were Brenda's sister and her husband and son, who were from Houston. Counting Ben Roy and Hildegarde (Brenda's parents), there were eight of us in all. In a fit of holiday madness, we all crowded into that one room, which served as kitchen, living room, and bedroom. Not infrequently, both Leah and her cousin Scott would invite a friend, bringing the total number of occupants to ten.

The obvious overcrowding and inconvenience were far outweighed by the sense of family we enjoyed. Our only entertainment was what we provided for ourselves. Consequently, we spent the long evenings playing games, singing songs, and swapping family history. It was here that Leah learned about the Great Depression, about life in the forties during the "Big War," with its shortages and ration cards, and about her grandparents' courtship.

Brenda's father is an early riser, and I often awaken to the small sounds he makes stirring up the fire. Soon the rich aroma of brewing coffee coaxes me fully awake. As the cabin grows warm, Ben Roy and I talk, while around us the rest of the family sleeps peacefully.

On Thanksgiving Day, a host of friends and relatives usually drive in. It is not unusual to have as many as fifty or sixty people for dinner. The big event, other than Thanksgiving dinner of course, is the annual touch football game. We call it the Vallew Bowl, and we do battle in the pasture. Fittingly, the game's most valuable player wins one thousand cow patties!

There are horseshoe tournaments for the "old" guys and rocking chairs on the porch for the grandmas. The kids explore the woods in the creek bottom, play hide-n-seek in the barn, and frolic on the homemade swing that soars over the pond twenty feet below.

By nightfall, we are all pleasantly tired, uncomfortably sore, and more than ready to gather around the bonfire in the yard. After we have eaten our fill of Thanksgiving leftovers and roasted marshmallows, we share a time of worship and thanksgiving before calling it a day for another year.

♥ *Love in Action*

Identify some of your family traditions. Make a commitment to God and each other that you will preserve them for your children.

♡♡ *Thought for the Day*

"Family traditions are the threads which link one generation to the next."

— Richard Exley

♡♡ *Scripture for the Day*

Impress them on your children. Talk about them when you sit at home and when you walk along the road, when you lie down and when you get up. Tie them as symbols on your hands and bind them on your foreheads. Write them on the doorframes of your houses and on your gates.

— Deuteronomy 6:7-9

♡♡ *Prayer*

Lord, we thank You for the rich heritage our parents have given to us. Enable us to pass it on to our children. In Jesus' name we pray. Amen.

chapter 32

♡♡♡♡

Personal Wholeness

*P*ersons who are unhappy, wounded, or bitter find it almost impossible to build a lasting marriage. Because of their past hurts and disappointments, they continually misinterpret and overreact, thus destroying the very thing they most desire — emotionally intimacy.

"How," you may be wondering, "can I tell if I am harboring some marriage-compromising hurt?" There are two basic clues. The first is found in your relationships. Did you have a troubled childhood? Do you currently have a good relationship with your parents and siblings? Are your current friendships healthy and long-standing, or do you have a history of volatile, short-term relationships?

Emotionally healthy people are usually the product of a good childhood, and their current relationships are healthy and long-lasting. Unwhole people, on the other hand, usually have a troubled family history and a pattern of volatile, short-term relationships.

The second clue is found in the way you respond to the vicissitudes of life. Is your response commensurate to the event that triggered it, or is it disproportionate? Emotionally healthy people demonstrate appropriate emotional responses, while wounded people tend to overreact or to manifest inappropriate emotions.

Let me illustrate. In the novel, *The Prince of Tides*, Tom Wingo uses humor to deal with both his pain and his anger. Casually he explains his behavior as "the southern way." But it is not the southern way. It is Tom Wingo's way. When something hurts too much, like his brother Luke's death, his twin sister's attempted suicide, or his childhood memories, he copes by being funny. Humor, however, is an inappropriate and unhealthy way of dealing with grief. As a result, Tom grows emotionally distant from those closest to him, including his wife.

Tom's inability to respond to Luke's death with the appropriate emotion is evidence of a far deeper dysfunction. And as the novel unfolds we are given glimpses into his terrifying childhood, a childhood marked by domestic violence, sexual abuse, and secrecy. And, as Tom tells his sister's psychiatrist, the secrecy is the worst.

It is no wonder then that he cannot be emotionally intimate with his wife. If he lets Sallie get too close to him, she might discover his secrets. Finally, his ambivalence ·toward her becomes unbearable, and she confronts him. This time she will not be put off by his humor or his self-pity.

"'It's hurting us, Tom.'"

"'I know.... To my surprise, I'm not a good husband. I once thought I'd be a great one. Charming, sensitive, loving, and attentive to my wife's every need. I'm sorry, Sallie. I haven't been good for you in such a long time. It's a source of great pain. I want to be better. I'm so cold, so secretive. I swear I'll do better...."'

"'You blame your parents for so much, Tom. When does it start becoming your own responsibility? When do you take your life into your own hands? When do you start accepting the blame or credit for your own actions?'"[1]

If, like Tom Wingo, you have discovered that your past, with its hurts and disappointments, has invaded your marriage, let me urge you to stop blaming others and take responsibility for your actions. With the help of a pastor or Christian counselor, you can overcome the past. You can be made whole. Then, and only then, will your marriage be all that you long for it to be.

💞 *Love in Action*

If you caught a glimpse of yourself or your marriage in this chapter, let me urge you to see your pastor or a Christian counselor. Emotional wholeness is foundational to a healthy marriage, therefore it is imperative that you get the help you need.

💞 *Thought for the Day*

"Perhaps your memories are painful.... Your past seems like a nuclear winter, desolate and frozen. Don't turn away! As painful as it may be, that too is who you are. Deny it, and you deny a part of yourself. Repress it, and you sentence yourself to a

lifetime of irrational responses and misdirected outbursts. Embrace it. Feel the pain. Shed the tears you have so long withheld. You are not alone. Jesus is with you, and He will redeem your past (that is, make it contribute to your ultimate Christlikeness)."[2]

— Richard Exley

♡♡ Scripture for the Day

The lamp of the LORD *searches the spirit of a man; it searches out his inmost being.*

— Proverbs 20:27

♡♡ Prayer

Lord, make me whole, that I may become the kind of spouse and parent You have called me to be. In Jesus' name I pray. Amen.

chapter 33

♡ ♡ ♡ ♡

Young Love

I was only six years old the first time I fancied myself in love. That was more than forty years ago, and try as I might I can't remember her name, the color of her eyes, or how she looked. I do remember the day she gave me a small gift-wrapped box, proudly announcing that she had bought it with her own money. Inside was a pair of cuff links and thirty-seven shiny copper pennies.

Having never seen any cuff links, I had no idea what to do with them. Finally, I decided to give them to my best friend. The pennies I kept. Every afternoon on the way home from school, I stopped by the corner store and treated myself to an infinite variety of penny candies. For nearly a month, the booty of love made me the richest kid on the block.

This was just the first in a series of young loves. In the sixth grade I fell hard for a pretty girl named Leah. That lasted until I went to church camp during summer vacation. There I lost my heart to a young lady with copper-colored hair. In time she was replaced by the girl I sat behind in my eighth-grade English class.

When I was sixteen, I went swimming in the South Platte River on a hot August afternoon with a pretty girl who would one day become my wife. Carelessly we splashed in the river, oblivious to the sun's deadly rays. Later that evening I rubbed Noxema skin cream on her sunburned shoulders, and to this day Noxema skin cream smells like love to me.

By now you are probably remembering your own young loves — and with a bit of chagrin no doubt. Don't be embarrassed. There is nothing wrong with puppy love — not if you are in the first grade, or the fifth grade, or even fifteen years old. The thing that concerns me, though, is that many couples never seem to outgrow their childish fantasies. Years later they continue to believe in Prince Charming, Cinderella, and living "happily ever after."

Unfortunately, life in the real world is not at all like a fairy tale. Prince Charming puts on twenty-five pounds and leaves his dirty clothes lying around. Cinderella discovers that homemaking isn't all that it is cracked up to be. With laundry, housecleaning, and child care, there is little time or energy left for being romantic. And on those rare occasions when she is feeling amorous, Prince Charming is engrossed in Monday night football or barricaded behind the evening paper.

Given this all too familiar scenario, many couples conclude that they don't love each other any more. In truth, only young love has died with its unrealistic expectations. If they can accept this fact and move past it, they will likely discover a new and deeper love. It will be a more mature love, based on real commitment, rather than mere emotion.

♡♡ *Love in Action*

Make a commitment to consistently give your marriage priority time and energy. That is true love, and it is the stuff of which real marriages are made.

♡♡ *Thought for the Day*

"Marriage is in trouble today because society and the church have a faulty view of it, a myth of this human, delightful, yet flawed, institution. Though a few lone voices speak against the institution, most laud a romantic image of marriage as life's ultimate source of true joy."[1]

— Frederick Herwaldt, Jr.

♡♡ *Scripture for the Day*

Jacob was in love with Rachel and said [to her father], "I'll work for you seven years in return for your younger daughter Rachel.' Laban said, 'It's better that I give her to you than to some other man. Stay here with me." So Jacob served seven years to get Rachel, but they seemed like only a few days to him because of his love for her.

— Genesis 29:18-20

♡♡ *Prayer*

Lord, help us to lay aside childish things like young love, with its emphasis on emotion and self-gratification. Grant us a true love, one that is both selfless and unconditional. In Your Holy name we pray. Amen.

chapter 34

For Better or For Worse

"*I* can't take it any more," Lisa says, her voice sounding dead. "Whatever love we once shared is long gone. We don't even care enough to fight."

Looking miserable, Dave nods his head in agreement. "We simply don't have anything in common."

Although I sense their unhappiness, I cannot help wondering what three children, a shared faith in Jesus Christ, and nearly twenty years of marriage are, if not things in common.

Putting my elbows on the desk, I rest my chin on my hands and study them intently before finally saying, "So?"

For a moment neither of them respond, their disappointment visible in their faces. Finally Lisa finds her voice. "Is that all you have to say?" she demands, with more than a hint of anger. "We tell you our marriage is over, and all you can say is 'So'?"

Turning to Dave I ask, "In your wedding vows was there anything like 'for richer or poorer, in sickness and in health, till death do us part'?"

Looking puzzled, he nods.

"Lisa," I ask, "can you remember anything about 'for better or for worse'?"

"Of course," she snaps. "Doesn't everyone say that when they get married?"

"Well," I ask, "what did you think worse was?"

Slowly it dawns on them. They have made a vow to God, for better or for worse, and I am holding them accountable.

"Surely," Dave asks, "God doesn't expect us to spend the rest of our lives being miserable?"

"Absolutely not!" I reply. "But neither is divorce the answer."

I have their attention now, so I continue. "Experience has taught me that there is enough disappointment and pain in the best of marriages to tempt one with divorce if that were a scriptural option. By the same token, there is enough hope in the most miserable marriage to justify hanging in there. In truth, there is no marriage that God cannot heal if both partners will surrender unconditionally to the Lordship of Jesus Christ, and fully commit themselves to each other."

"It won't be easy," I continue, "but with God's help your marriage can become all you ever hoped it would be."

Dave and Lisa are skeptical. To their way of thinking, there are only two options — continue the status quo or divorce. The possibility of rediscovering love and happiness in their own marriage has never occurred to them.

However, after much soul-searching, they decide to give it one more try.

It isn't easy, but with God's help they are able to reconnect with each other. Dave learns to be more assertive, thus fulfilling his responsibilities as the family leader. Outspoken by nature, Lisa determines to be affirming, rather than critical. As a result, Dave comes out of his shell and begins to communicate. Over a period of months their marriage is restored.

♡ *Love in Action*

Get a copy of your wedding vows and review them together. Talk specifically about what they mean. Reaffirm your commitment to each other and the vows you made.

♡ *Thought for the Day*

"And the thing that neither one of us would even contemplate was divorce. We were stuck with each other. Let the world call that imprisonment; but I say it gave us the time, and God the opportunity, to make a better thing between us. If we could have escaped, we would have. Because we couldn't, we were forced to choose the harder, better road." [1]

— Walter Wangerin, Jr.

♡♡ Scripture for the Day

...So guard yourself in your spirit, and do not break faith with the wife [husband] of your youth. "I hate divorce," says the LORD God of Israel, "and I hate a man's [woman's] covering himself [herself] with violence as well as with his [her] garment," says the LORD Almighty. So guard yourself in your spirit, and do not break faith.

— Malachi 2:15,16

♡♡ Prayer

Lord, we renew the marriage covenant we have made with You. We promise You that we will love and cherish each other all the days of our lives — for better or for worse, for richer or poorer, in sickness and in health, till death do us part. In Your Holy name we pray. Amen.

chapter 35

♡ ♡ ♡ ♡

Affair-Proofing Your Marriage

*U*npremeditated affairs are usually birthed in an unfulfilling marriage; consequently, if you can make your marriage all God intends it to be, you can minimize the risks of infidelity. With that thought in mind, let me share some guidelines that have served my wife and me well these past thirty years. We call them the "Ten Commandments for a Healthy Marriage."

Commandment # 1: Protect your day off at all costs and spend it together, as a couple, and as a family. If an emergency makes it impossible for you to have your regularly scheduled time together, reschedule another day immediately. Nothing is more important than the time you spend together.

Commandment # 2: Eat dinner together. Even when you have a simple meal, make it an occasion by lighting candles and turning off the TV. Dinner conversation is a time for sharing and making memories. Issues can be dealt with at another time.

Commandment # 3: Go to bed together. Nothing undermines intimacy faster than separate bedtimes. This is a time for touching and sharing. It's an opportunity to touch base with each other, to make sure you haven't let your hectic schedules cause you to drift apart. Without these "set times" for togetherness, you may lose contact with each other in the "busyness" of life.

Commandment # 4: Don't hold a grudge. If you insist on nursing yesterday's hurts, you will become prematurely old and bitter, forfeiting any chance you have of enjoying each other. We've all been hurt by those we love most, some of us more than others, I'll grant you that. Nevertheless, the only hope for your marriage lies in your ability to forgive and forget. Don't let past hurts rob you of today's joy!

Commandment # 5: Don't take separate vacations. Shared experiences bond you together, while unshared experiences distance you from one another. Time is one of the most valuable commodities in your marriage, so spend it wisely.

Commandment # 6: Never let anything rob your marriage of the sexual joy God intended. Sex is a gift from God to be enjoyed within the holy bonds of marriage. It is designed as a means of expressing love and giving pleasure, as well as for procreation. While true intimacy is more than sex, it is never less than that.

Commandment # 7: Pray together. Nothing is more intimate than a personal relationship with God. When you invite your spouse to share that experience with you, you are opening the deepest part of your being to him or her. It can be threatening at first, but the rewards more than justify the effort.

Commandment # 8: Play together. K. C. Cole, reporting in *Psychology Today*, writes: "All happy couples aren't alike, so there is no single litmus test for a good marriage. But if one studies couples systematically over time, it becomes apparent that many of them share a characteristic that signals, more often than not, a healthy union.

"It's nothing so obvious as a satisfying sexual relationship, or shared interests, or the habit of talking out disputes freely. It is, rather, a capacity for playfulness of a kind that transcends fun and reflects considerably more than the partners' ability to amuse each other. Private nicknames, shared jokes and fantasies, mock insults, make-believe fighting — all these might seem like mere silliness. In fact, they may stand in for, or lubricate, more complex transactions, essential but potentially painful or even destructive."[1]

Commandment # 9: Pay attention to the little things; they mean a lot. In fact, they can make the difference between a mediocre marriage and a really good one. It's usually not the expensive gifts or the foreign vacations that determine the quality of a marital relationship, but the little things. A love note in his lunch box or an "unbirthday" card for her. A kind word, help with the children, a listening ear, the feeling that he or she really cares.

Commandment # 10: Pledge yourselves, not only to physical faithfulness, but to emotional fidelity as well. Determine that your emotional needs will be fulfilled only in your marriage. Do not allow friends, family, or career to supply these "belonging needs." Provide these for each other, and it will be the strength of your relationship.

Maintaining a healthy marriage does not eliminate temptation, but it does minimize its impact. When your deepest spiritual and emotional needs are met in relationship with God and your spouse, you can respond as a whole person to those who seek your friendship and support. Since your emotional needs are being fulfilled in appropriate ways, you will not need to use extramarital friendships as a means for establishing your value as a person. You may still be tempted, but now you can respond out of wholeness rather than need.

❧ *Love in Action*

Spend a few minutes with your spouse discussing these ten commandments. Explore ways to integrate them more fully into your own marriage.

❧ *Thought for the Day*

"...marriage is both a gift and a discipline. God gives us each other and the tools for cultivating our blessed oneness, but it is up to us to work the soil of our relationship all the days of our lives."[2]

— Richard Exley

❧ *Scripture for the Day*

Above all else, guard your heart, for it is the wellspring of life.

— Proverbs 4:23

❧ *Prayer*

Lord, make our marriage God-centered and our family marriage-centered. In the name of Jesus we pray. Amen.

chapter 36

Help for the Hard of Hearing

The house is deathly still as I enter the kitchen from the garage. The usual aroma of dinner is absent, as is the familiar fire in the fireplace. I experience a moment of uneasiness as I turn toward the staircase leading to the bedrooms. After twenty years of marriage, I am accustomed to Brenda's routines. She is an orderly woman, and this is not like her.

Nearing the top of the stairs, I hear the sound of sobbing coming from the master bedroom. In an instant I imagine the worst. My father has just undergone open-heart surgery, and I am sure he has died. Bursting into the bedroom, I ask, "Has something happened to Dad? Is he all right?"

Wiping her tears, Brenda manages to assure me that my father is fine, but she cannot stop crying. Helplessly, I watch as she turns toward the wall, seeming to shrink within herself, all the while sobbing piteously. Sitting down beside her, I put my arm around her shoulders, but she does not turn to me, nor does she seem to take comfort from my presence.

Slowly her sobs subside and finally cease altogether. At last she turns to me, and I venture a tentative question. "Can you talk about it?" I ask. "Can you tell me what is troubling you?"

For a long time she doesn't say anything. When she finally speaks, in a voice sounding sad and old, I have to strain to catch her words. With great trepidation she pours out her hurts and fears, her self-doubts.

Two years removed from a terrible automobile accident, she is still in constant pain. Always an immaculate housekeeper, she can no longer keep her house the way she once did. It is spotlessly clean by anyone's standards but her own, but still she is depressed. Leah, our only child, is nearing graduation, and Brenda cannot bear the thought of her leaving home. For eighteen years Brenda has been a full-time mother, and now she is facing the empty nest. And worst of all — I don't understand her.

I am stunned by the depth of her feelings. How could I have been so blind to her pain? I have been busy doing the work of the ministry, but that is no excuse. The woman I love most in all the world has been dying right before my eyes, and I have not seen it.

Although I want to defend myself, I cannot. The proof of my selfishness and insensitivity sits weeping before me. With bowed head I listen as Brenda enumerates my shortcomings. True, all true.

In retrospect it all seems so obvious. For years I have frustrated her with advice and exhortations. Anytime she tried to share a problem with me, I always had a ready answer. Unfortunately, what she sought was not my "wisdom," but my understanding. My easy answers and constant advice, she said, only made her feel silly and inadequate. As a consequence, she chose to suffer alone with her hurt, being careful to hide it from me, for I had not proved worthy of her trust.

This time I do not try to "fix" anything. I offer no advice, no exhortation to do better. For once I simply listen, allowing Brenda's pain and aloneness to become my own. I am grieved, for her depression is at least partially my fault; still, I must not succumb to self-pity. This is Brenda's time, and I must not let regret blind me to her need.

After her grief has spent itself, we sit for a long time in loving silence. Painful though it is, I am thankful for what has transpired. I sense that we have turned a corner. If I can continue to listen with compassion and understanding, perhaps Brenda can learn to trust me with her feelings again. Perhaps we can finally learn to truly communicate.

♡ *Love in Action*

Ask your spouse to help you become a compassionate listener. Give him/her permission to begin a conversation by saying something like: "I am not asking for advice or suggestions right now. I just need for you to listen to me and to try to understand what I am feeling."

♡ *Thought for the Day*

"It is thus vain to hope to understand one's husband or wife without listening long, and with great interest.... The essential part...is listening, long and passionate listening, with love and respect and with a real effort at understanding."[1]

— Paul Tournier

♡ *Scripture for the Day*

Do not be quick with your mouth, do not be hasty in your heart to utter anything before God. God is in heaven and you are on earth, so let your words be few. As a dream comes when there are many cares, so the speech of a fool when there are many words.

— Ecclesiastes 5:2,3

♡ *Prayer*

Lord, help me not to seek to be understood, rather let me seek to be understanding. Let me begin by understanding my mate. In Your Holy name I pray. Amen.

chapter 37
♡ ♡ ♡ ♡

The Tender Trap

*C*ontrary to popular belief, most extramarital affairs begin for non-sexual reasons. The lack of need fulfillment and intimacy creates an intense vacuum, making the desire for emotional intimacy the primary reason why people have an affair. Many a shocked husband has said, after discovering that his wife is having an affair, "What does she see in him?" His wife's response? "He listens, cares, and he doesn't criticize me!"

When the need for closeness, goodness, kindness, and togetherness — what I call our "ness" needs — is not being met on a regular basis in a marriage, the temptation may be to find a person who will be good to us, touch us, hold us, and give us a feeling of closeness. Sexual fulfillment may become an important part of an extramarital relationship, but the "ness" needs are, for most men and women, initially more important.

What am I trying to say? Simply this: An innocent get-together like working with each other on a project, helping a neighbor, or even meeting for coffee, can begin a pattern of meetings that become increasingly mutually fulfilling. Soon the parties are sharing deeply, which gives birth to emotional intimacy, which, inexorably, leads to adultery. As one man put it, "In two weeks we were in bed together. I just can't believe it's happening to me!"

For others the journey into the pitfalls of adultery begins with some "innocent flirting" that is carefully couched in double meanings. If the one being flirted with fails to respond or becomes offended, the person doing the flirting can protest his innocence, claiming he was misunderstood. On the other hand, if the "flirtee" responds in kind, the chase is on, and excitement is high. Neither person has yet made a conscious decision to commit adultery, but subconsciously they are committed to it.

Once this deadly descent begins, it rapidly advances from one stage to the next. Now, the potential adulterers spend significant amounts of time fantasizing about each other. As the "affair" progresses, these fantasies become more explicit. For the man, they will often be sexual in nature, though not always; while for the woman, they will usually be romantic.

During the next stage they find excuses for calling each other. And they will spend extended periods of time in deep conversations — often about spiritual things or personal problems. They will create legitimate reasons for spending time with one another — a special project at work or a church program — anything that allows them to be together.

By this time they are actively committing adultery, not physically, but emotionally; that is, they are getting their "ness" needs met by someone other than their spouse. Someone other than their spouse is satisfying their need for closeness, tenderness, and togetherness.

Now they begin to justify their relationship. First, they carefully catalog every failure in their marriage. They recite their spouse's shortcomings in deadly detail. They remember and magnify every problem. Their spouse is insensitive and unresponsive. Surely God doesn't expect them to live their entire lives in such an unhappy state. With a little help from such rationalization, their compatibility leads smoothly into tenderness, the tenderness to a need for privacy, the privacy to physical consolation, and the consolation straight to bed.

Once they physically commit adultery, they find themselves in a maelstrom of emotions. Guilt and fear haunt them. Their self-esteem falters. They live with the constant fear of being found out. Prayer seems impossible. How can they face God? Yet even as they writhe in remorse, they are driven with excitement and desire. They hate what they are doing, but they feel powerless to stop. They vow to break it off, to go back to just being friends, but to no avail. Their good intentions are just that — good intentions — nothing more. Like moths drawn irresistibly to a flame, they seem destined to self-destruct.

As the affair progresses, their excitement wears off while their guilt and fear increase. Now they feel trapped. There is no way out of the relationship without hurting the other person, yet they can't continue like this indefinitely either. No matter what they do now, someone is going to get hurt, and hurt badly!

Now they must face the spouse they have betrayed, the children they have abandoned, and the God they have disobeyed. The consequences are inevitable:

"Can a man scoop fire into his lap without his clothes being burned?

"Can a man walk on hot coals without his feet being scorched?

"So is he who sleeps with another man's wife; no one who touches her will go unpunished. ...a man who commits adultery lacks judgment; whoever does so destroys himself."[1]

If you have caught a glimpse of your marriage as you have read this, now is the time to take corrective action. Give your marriage first priority. Invest time and energy in the relationship. Determine to meet each other's "ness" needs. If you don't know where to start, seek competent counsel from a minister or a Christian marriage counselor.

♡ *Love in Action*

If there is anything dangerous or inappropriate about any relationship in your life, confess it to God and renounce it. Terminate the relationship immediately, and make yourself accountable to a trusted friend or to your pastor.

♡♡ *Thought for the Day*

"Men, put disciplined hedges around your life — especially if you work with women. Refrain from verbal intimacy with women other than your spouse. Do not bare your heart to another woman, or pour forth your troubles to her. Intimacy is a great need in most people's lives — and talking about personal matters, especially one's problems, can fill another's need of intimacy, awakening a desire for more. Many affairs begin in just this way."[2]

— R. Kent Hughes

♡♡ *Scripture for the Day*

You shall not commit adultery.

— Exodus 20:14

♡♡ *Prayer*

Lord, make us especially sensitive to meet each other's emotional needs. Build a hedge around our marriage. Protect our hearts from the evil one. In Your Holy name we pray. Amen.

chapter 38

The Moment of Maybe

"Early on in an extramarital friendship," writes Walter Wangerin Jr., "there often comes a moment of 'maybe.' Even when that friendship is altogether innocent, your friend may send the signal, or you may sense the feeling, of further possibility. It occurs in a glance more meaningful than mere friends exchange. It arises from a touch, a hug, a brushing of flesh that tingled rather more than you expected — and you remembered the sensation.... In that moment nothing more is communicated than this: our friendship could turn into something else. Neither of you need say, or even think, what that 'something else' might be.... It is precisely here that the drama toward adultery begins. Whether it also ends here, or whether it continues hereafter, is a terribly critical question. For a door has opened up.

"If, in this moment, you do nothing at all, then you enter the door. If you make no decision (privately but consciously) to close the door and carefully to restrict this relationship, the drama continues. For though a promise has not been made in the moment of 'maybe,' it hasn't been denied either. And though you may not yet love each other, neither have you said no to love. You permit, by making no decision at all, the 'maybe.' And 'maybe' takes on a life of its own."[1]

Wangerin concludes: "When a desire is born in us, we have a choice. When it exists still in its infancy, we have a choice. We can carefully refuse its existence altogether, since it needs our complicity to exist.... Or else we can attend to it, think about it, fantasize it into greater existence — feed it! But, if we do the latter, if we give it attention in our souls, soon we will be giving it our souls. We've lost free will and the opportunity to choose. The desire itself overpowers us, commanding action, demanding satisfaction."[2]

Since temptation is so subtle, you may protest, it is not always easy to recognize a moment of "maybe." True enough, especially if you are inclined toward rationalization.

In your defense, you reason that being a Christian friend requires you to be sensitive, supportive, and caring. And it does, but there is a point where your concern becomes more than friendship, a point at which you find yourself meeting emotional needs for each other that can be met legitimately only by one's spouse. Although you haven't yet done anything sexually inappropriate, you are, nonetheless, guilty of emotional adultery. And if you do not take immediate steps to rectify the situation, it is only a matter of time until you will find yourself entangled in a full-blown affair.

♥ *Love in Action*

Invite the Holy Spirit to examine your heart and your relationships in light of the "moment of maybe."

♥ *Thought for the Day*

"The only time to stop temptation is at the first point of recognition. If one begins to argue and engage in a hand-to-hand combat, temptation almost always wins the day."[3]

— Thomas à Kempis

♥ *Scripture for the Day*

But among you there must not be even a hint of sexual immorality, or of any kind of impurity....

— Ephesians 5:3

♥ *Prayer*

Lord, redeem my sexual desires, sanctify them, make them a pure and holy gift to my spouse. In the name of Jesus I pray. Amen.

chapter 39

♡ ♡ ♡

When the Vow Breaks

Glaring at her husband, Esther said, "You think you know me, but you don't!"

"Maybe not," he replied, shaking his head, "but God knows I've tried."

"Dale," she said, anger giving way to a tired sadness, "you don't want to know me. You want to control me. You want to tell me what to think and how to feel."

When he still seemed baffled, she tried again. "You run my whole life, and you have for thirty years. The only part of me that is mine is what I keep from you."

As their pastor, I found their situation especially sad. They were both Christians and leaders in the church, yet after thirty years of marriage Esther had become involved with another man. In retrospect, her affair seems nearly inevitable. She hadn't been happy in years, nor had she been able to talk about it. In truth, she had just been waiting for something to happen, for just the right person to come along. If it had not been Brad, it would have been someone else, of that I was sure.

Dale was a good man, but as Esther said, a controlling one, and very much like her father in that respect. As a child, Esther had learned to say and do "right" things rather than "real" things, lest she suffer her father's disapproval. On the inside, however, she had lived a secret life with her own ideas and values. When she married, she simply transferred this unhealthy way of relating from her father to her husband.

Complicating matters was Dale's explosive temper. Over the years it had taken its toll. One day Esther realized that she didn't love Dale anymore, and hadn't for a long time. Even then, she did not consider divorce. Instead, she sought fulfillment in other areas — her children, her friends, and her work. She continued to perform her wifely duties as if she was not dying on the inside. Dale was blind to it all, never noticing that Esther was emotionally distancing herself from him.

When circumstances thrust Esther into a working relationship with Brad, she found herself enjoying his company in a way she had never enjoyed being with her husband. Brad respected her opinions and never tried to tell her what to think. For the first time in her life, she was with a man who did not try to dominate her. With Brad she felt safe, safe enough to be her real self.

Of course, it was only a matter of time until they were confiding in each other, which created an emotional bond, which in turn lead to sexual intimacy. Since both of them were married and Christians, they hated what they were doing but seemed powerless to stop. On several occasions they vowed to end their infidelity, to return to just being friends, only to discover that once the barriers to intimacy have been breached they are almost impossible to restore. Because they worked together, it was impossible to completely terminate the relationship without creating a financial hardship, not to mention the risk involved in explaining such a decision.

Esther and Brad continued in their self-made trap for several months. Finally, she could bear her guilt no more and in desperation confessed everything to her husband. She fully expected it to end their marriage. Even if Dale did not demand a divorce, she knew that she could not live the rest of her life a prisoner of his anger. To Esther's fearful surprise, he wanted to forgive her and restore their marriage. It was a frightening prospect. The last thing she wanted to do was to fall back into the trap that her marriage had become. She couldn't imagine spending the rest of her life in a loveless union, nor could she continue to pretend to be something she was not in order to be accepted by her husband.

It was a fearful thing for Dale too. He wondered if he could ever trust her again. Could he change? Could he learn to control his verbal outbursts? Could he accept her as a person in her own right and not just an extension of himself? Could she learn to express her real feelings even at the risk of a confrontation? Could their marriage truly be restored? These and a thousand other questions tormented him day and night.

In desperation they sought my pastoral counsel.

I could not help thinking how different things might have been had either of them recognized what was happening in their marriage and sought outside help. For them such speculation is pointless, but for you and your spouse it may prove invaluable. Not only does early detection prevent unhealthy behaviors from becoming lifelong habits, it has the added benefit of avoiding the painful tragedy of infidelity, which is almost always the consequence of ignoring marital difficulties.

♡♡ *Love in Action*

Carefully examine your heart to see if there are any hidden resentments or feelings of anger toward your spouse. Don't sweep your feelings under the rug. They won't go away unless you resolve the issues that are generating them. If you cannot resolve these issues together, then seek outside help — from either a pastor or a Christian counselor.

♡ *Thought for the Day*

"There is no broken marriage that God cannot heal if we will give Him all the pieces."

— Richard Exley

♡ *Scripture for the Day*

...Go, show your love to your wife again, though she is loved by another and is an adulteress. Love her as the LORD loves the Israelites, though they turn to other gods....

— Hosea 3:1

♡ *Prayer*

Lord, give those who have known the terrible pain of infidelity the strength of Your Holy love, to forgive, to trust again, and to begin anew. In the name of Jesus I pray. Amen.

chapter 40

♡ ♡ ♡ ♡

Healing Grace

*N*o marriage is beyond the reach of God's healing grace. If both spouses will make an unconditional commitment to their marriage and to the Lordship of Jesus Christ, their relationship can be restored. It won't happen instantaneously, and it won't be easy. But, it is possible, as Esther and Dale learned.

Initially, each of them was tempted to blame the other. Esther blamed Dale for her infidelity. If he had not been so controlling, if he had not been given to verbal outbursts, if he had been more sensitive to her needs and desires.... The list went on and on. As her pastor, I helped her to understand that while Dale's behavior contributed to her unhappiness, he did not cause her to be unfaithful. That was her choice, her way of responding to her pain and unhappiness.

It was even harder for her to accept that her way of reacting to Dale's verbal outbursts and controlling manner was also her choice. He did not make her hide her true feelings and opinions. She chose to do that because it was easier than risking a confrontation. It was a natural choice for her, one that she learned early in her childhood, but a poor one nonetheless.

Taking responsibility for his part in the wounding of their marriage was no less difficult for Dale. That Esther considered him a verbally abusive man was almost more than he could imagine. Sure, he got angry from time to time, but that was no big thing — just his way of dealing with stress. Besides, he always apologized. Didn't that count for something?

To his way of thinking, his good deeds more than made up for his angry outbursts. From Esther's perspective, they were empty acts. "I didn't think he meant them," she explained. "If he really loved me, how could he become so angry at me? How could he scream at me one minute and in the very next breath tell me what a wonderful wife I was? It didn't make sense to me. I couldn't trust my emotions to him. Even if he went days between angry outbursts, I knew it was just a matter of time until it happened again."

When I asked her if she ever tried to tell Dale how she felt, she said: "I couldn't. Dale is a far better talker than I am. Any time we argued he always made me feel like it was all my fault. He made me feel like a bad person, and I hated that feeling."

Thankfully, both Esther and Dale were committed to their marriage and were willing to invest the time and energy necessary to see it restored. Both eventually accepted their part in the terrible tragedy that had befallen them, and over a period of months they were able to develop healthier ways of relating to each other. The task before them was a difficult one, strewn with many pitfalls, but at least they were willing to begin the rebuilding of their marriage.

♡ *Love in Action*

After reading about Esther and Dale, do you recognize any unhealthy ways in which you and your spouse relate to each other? What changes, if any, do you need to make? Be specific.

♡ *Thought for the Day*

"'I have to hurt you,' she said. The strident voice had turned to whining by now. She wasn't shouting any more. She was just unspeakably sad. 'I had to hurt you to make you notice me. I hate it. I hate it!... At least I know it when I hurt you. You don't even know.'"[1]

— Walter Wangerin, Jr.

♡ *Scripture for the Day*

If an enemy were insulting me, I could endure it; if a foe were raising himself against me, I could hide from him.

But it is you, a man like myself, my companion, my close friend.

— Psalm 55:12,13

♡♡ Prayer

Lord, all is not lost. Where sin does abound, grace does even more abound. What sin has destroyed, You can heal and restore. Come quickly, O Lord, and do Your healing work. In the name of Jesus we pray. Amen.

chapter 41

Making Peace With the Past

*W*hen Dale learned of Esther's affair, he was devastated. In an instant his comfortable world was destroyed. At first her confession made no sense. He understood her words, but shock and denial rendered them unreal. This couldn't be happening to him, to them — not after more than thirty years of marriage. Then the pain hit him, driving him to his knees, reducing his breathing to a strangled wheeze. Finally, he managed a choking whisper, "Why didn't you just take a gun and shoot me? It would have been kinder."

The anger came later, wave after wave of it. And an overwhelming feeling of helplessness. No matter what he did, there was no way to change what had happened. It made no sense to him. How could she do something like this? It went against everything she was, against everything she believed. Grief, greater than anything he had ever experienced, convulsed him. For hours sobs racked his body.

Well do I remember his initial telephone call. "Pastor," he said, his voice choked with pain, "Esther's having an affair."

When I asked him what he planned to do, he replied, "I've thought about jumping off a cliff, but I don't suppose that's a very good idea." After a short pause he continued, "I need to talk to you. I need some help to sort all of this out."

In our early one-on-one sessions, Dale poured out his grief and anger. In explicit detail he told me what he would like to do to Esther's lover. Though I had never heard this Christian man curse, his language was now punctuated with profanity. Yet, even in his anger, he wanted to save his marriage, he wanted to see his relationship with Esther restored.

Patiently, I helped him move from anger to forgiveness.

"Forgiveness is an act of your will," I explained. "You begin by telling God how you really feel, that you don't want to forgive Esther, but that, in obedience to His Word, you are choosing to do it anyway. Give God permission to change your feelings, to replace your hurt and anger with a new love for Esther. Then you must forgive her specifically for each sin she committed against you and your marriage."

"What do you mean?" he asked.

"Well, you might pray something like this: 'God, with Your help, I choose to forgive Esther for lying to me about her relationship with Brad. I choose to let go of my hurt and anger.

"'God, with Your help, I choose to forgive Esther for betraying our wedding vows when she had sex with Brad. I choose to let go of my of my hatred and disgust.'"

"Dale," I continued, "you were not sinned against generally but specifically, therefore you must forgive each sinful act specifically."

Finally, he nodded and, in a voice I had to strain to hear, he began, "God, You know that the very thought of the things Esther did with that man makes me sick. When I look at her, I keep imagining them together. Sometimes I just want to run away, so I never have to see her again, but I can't. I want to forgive her, but I want to get even too. I want to hurt her the way she has hurt me, but I know that's not right. Please God, help me to forgive her."

Taking a deep breath, he prayed, "God, I choose to forgive Esther for having sex with Brad. I choose to forgive her for betraying me and the covenant of our marriage...."

Dale prayed for a long time that afternoon, dealing with one painful incident after another, and when he finally finished I knew their marriage could be healed. Not only was he willing to forgive Esther, but equally important, he was willing to address his destructive outbursts and his unhealthy need to control her.

The healing of their marriage was terribly hard work and often painfully slow. Along the way there were several crises. More than once Dale fell back into his old pattern of intimidation and control, causing Esther to withdraw in angry silence. Still, they were both committed to the healing of their marriage and, as the weeks turned into months, they began to discover a depth of love and intimacy they had never known.

♡♡ *Love in Action*

Search your heart and see if there is any unforgiveness there. If so, honestly confess your feelings to God in prayer. Now specifically let go of your hurt and forgive those who have sinned against you, especially your spouse.

♡♡ *Thought for the Day*

"The heart has a memory too, and it must be allowed to feel its pain fully before releasing its hold on the past.... Letting go is necessary if one is to find release from the pain. Letting go allows one to flow forward again with the movement of time, to be present once more with oneself, one's companions, one's universe."[1]

— David Augsburger

♡♡ *Scripture for the Day*

Forgive us our sins, for we also forgive everyone who sins against us....

— Luke 11:4

♡ *Prayer*

Lord, remind us of Your great mercy so that we may be merciful toward each other and everyone else. Baptize us in Your unconditional love so that we may find the grace to forgive one another and all those who have sinned against us. In the name of Jesus we pray. Amen.

chapter 42

Starting Over

I watched as my freshly refilled cup of coffee steamed, then stopped steaming, then grew cold. All the while Dale regaled me with the painful details of Esther's adultery. He needed someone with whom he could process his feelings, I knew that, but enough was enough. I had heard all of it before, and it was time for him to move on.

"Dale," I said, leaning across the table toward him, "infidelity is inexcusable, and it cannot be tolerated within marriage. But having said that, let me remind you that you must not define your marriage only by that tragic event."

"What do you mean?" he asked.

Taking a deep breath, I continued, "In the same way a severe toothache can make you unaware of how good the rest of your body feels, so a painful tragedy, like an affair, can make you temporarily blind to the positive benefits of your marriage. To get past this, you must make a conscious effort to remember the good times, the special moments in the life of your family. These too are a part of your marriage. The affair is an unspeakable tragedy, but it is only a tiny part of your shared life. In time it will become nothing more than a fading memory, a tragic reminder of our sinful humanity."

Dale nodded his head slowly, and I thought maybe I had gotten through to him. After paying for our coffee, we bid each other good-bye.

I didn't see Dale and Esther again for nearly two months. He had six weeks of vacation time coming, so they decided to go to a Christian retreat center which specialized in helping couples in crisis. They called once, near the end of their vacation, to give me an update. The sessions, they said, with both the counselor and the group were helpful, but nothing was more beneficial than the many hours they were spending together. They were taking long walks, basking in the quiet beauty of God's creation. Together, they were reading books, searching for some understanding of how this could have happened to them. They were sharing the Scriptures and praying together.

When I murmured my approval, they told me that they had shed a lot of tears as God's healing grace released their sorrows and healed their hearts. Slowly they were learning to trust again, and with it there was a restoration of their love for one another.

"For the first time ever I am beginning to see myself through Esther's eyes," Dale reported, "and it is not pretty. I have always thought of myself as a good man, affectionate and helpful. Esther recognized these qualities but, for her, they were dwarfed by my anger. From her perspective, our whole relationship was defined by my anger and my need to control her. She was afraid of me and, as we all know, you cannot long love someone you fear."

"It meant a lot to me," Esther confided, "when Dale finally acknowledged how his anger had terrorized our relationship. For the first time I began to take hope. Maybe our marriage could really be different. Maybe I could learn to love him again."

She paused for a moment, and when she continued there was a wistful tone in her voice. "The first time I heard him pray and ask God to guard his lips I thought, 'What a cop out.' But as he continued to pray the same prayer day after day, I began to notice a change. The angry Dale was gone, and in his place was a kinder, gentler man."

When I didn't say anything, she hastened to add: "He's not perfect yet, but God is really doing a work in his life."

Hanging up the telephone, I experienced a moment of joy. They were going to make it, of that I was sure. They still had a lot of work to do, but I sensed that they had turned a corner.

♡♡ *Love in Action*

On a scale of one to ten, with ten being the highest, rate the level of trust in your marriage. Compare your rating with that of your spouse. Identify at least three specific ways you can improve trust in your relationship.

♡ *Thought for the Day*

"Affairs are never right and never a good way to build a better marriage. But as good can come out of evil, so benefits can come from affairs, even though there are less painful and less sinful ways to accomplish these same purposes."[1]

— Henry A. Virkler, Ph.D.

♡ *Scripture for the Day*

Though you have made me see troubles, many and bitter, you will restore my life again; from the depths of the earth you will again bring me up. You will increase my honor and comfort me once again.

— Psalm 71:20,21

♡ *Prayer*

Lord, thank You for being with us in the hour of our unspeakable loss. Now give us the courage to trust again so that our marriage may be fully restored. In the name of Jesus we pray. Amen.

chapter 43

♡ ♡ ♡ ♡

Restoring Lost Love

*I*nfidelity is an unspeakable tragedy and a deadly wound, but it can also signal a new beginning for the marriage, a rebirth. When an adulterous affair becomes known, it sounds the death knell for the marriage. In some instances, the couple divorces, and the marriage is officially buried. In other cases, they may continue to live together, even though they have no relationship. Their marriage is dead, but not buried. And in some cases, when the old flawed marriage dies, a new, healthier marriage is born. This is what happened in the case of Esther and Dale.

Before they could have a true marriage, though, their old marriage had to die; it was flawed and unhealthy. Their old patterns of relating to each other, the way they communicated, even how they loved, were all tragically impaired. Esther's adultery made all of this painfully obvious, but instead of destroying them, it created a crisis which gave birth to a new beginning for both of them. As they opened their lives, and their marriage, to the work of the Holy Spirit, God began to transform their relationship.

Dale learned to love Esther in a new way. Previously, his love was suffocating. Well do I remember the day he finally realized this fact. "Esther was dying," he said, "not because I didn't love her, but because I loved her too much. She tried to tell me that I was smothering her, but I never understood what she meant."

Tears filled his eyes, and when he spoke again emotion made his voice thick. "A couple of nights ago we watched *Of Mice and Men*. Are you familiar with it?"

Nodding, I replied, "I read the novel years ago. It's by Steinbeck, I think."

"Then you know it's the story of two friends — George and Lennie — or maybe they are cousins. Lennie is simple, probably mentally retarded, a huge giant of a guy who doesn't know his own strength. George tries to look out for him, but Lennie is always messing things up. He's not mean; in fact, he seems to be tender-hearted in a simple sort of way. Unfortunately, he kills everything he loves — little rabbits, puppies, and ultimately the boss's wife. He doesn't mean to kill them, but not knowing his own strength, he squeezes them too tight. And even after they are dead, he goes right on petting them."

"Dale," I asked, "what are you telling me?"

Silent tears ran down his cheeks. "I'm like Lennie," he said, and his voice was fearfully sad. "I squeeze too tight.

That's what I did to Esther — I loved her to death. And even when she died, I never noticed. I just went on petting her."

Dale's pain was so obvious I wanted to take him in my arms and comfort him, but before I could, Esther reached over and took his hand. They looked at each other with tear-damp eyes. Finally, she said, "We're going to make it."

I couldn't help marveling at how far they had come. They hardly seemed like the same couple. The pain was still there, and it would be for a long time, but there was love there too, and hope. As Esther said, they were going to make it.

Frequently, I am asked, "Will I ever be able to love my wife again?" or, "After all that we've been through, will I ever be able to love my husband again?" The answer is yes! But it won't happen overnight, and it won't necessarily be easy. When love is restored, however, it will be especially true, for it will be a love born of adversity.

♡♡ *Love in Action*

Read 1 Corinthians 13:4-7. Now compare the way you love your spouse with the love described in these verses. Identify two or three specific ways to make your love for your spouse more like the scriptural model in 1 Corinthians 13.

♡♡ *Thought for the Day*

"Feelings of love usually wither and dry up in a sterile, dry environment. Love needs to be nurtured and fed. And when loving behaviors start to take place without pressure, the feelings of love are often rekindled.... The feelings of love can come back if they are nurtured by the behaviors of love."[1]

— Dr. David Stoop and Jan Stoop

♡♡ *Scripture for the Day*

Love never fails. But where there are prophecies, they will cease; where there are tongues, they will be stilled; where there is knowledge, it will pass away...now these three remain: faith, hope and love. But the greatest of these is love.

— 1 Corinthians 13:8,13

♡♡ *Prayer*

Lord, forgive our sinful failures. Heal our wounded souls. Restore our lost love and renew our marriage. In the name of Jesus we pray. Amen.

chapter 44

Rebuilding Trust

*W*hen you have sinned against your marriage seriously and repeatedly, saying you're sorry isn't enough. In order for your marriage to be healed, you must repent; that is, you have to change the way you manage your life, your marriage, and your career.

One man, whose marriage seemed doomed because of his workaholic habits, saw the light and did just that. Though he feared offending his wife by his businesslike approach, he nonetheless made appointments on his calendar to see her every day. He writes:

"...In the days that followed, I came home before dinner. A full hour before dinner. And I sat on a stool in the kitchen while Thanne cooked. And this is how I felt: artificial. The little talk we made was mostly forced, and Thanne was mostly silent.... She did love me. She had rediscovered it and told me so. But I don't think we were friends much.

"I kept coming home. Even when we didn't talk, I came. It was simple labor, the keeping of a covenant for its own sake, because it had been promised; there is no excitement in this part of the story.

"But the mere persistence of my presence caused Thanne to begin to trust me. If I was there yesterday, then I could be there tomorrow — therefore, she might risk a word or two today. And she did. Thanne began to talk. She began to believe that I would listen. And I did. The more she talked, the more I wanted to listen, and the more my own talk wasn't merely self-centered.

"It is a wonder when your beloved trusts you enough to give herself to you again, trusts you with her weight, her treasure, and her life....

"Now, though we may be separate in the morning, the ideas that occur to us apart we save for the hour when we will be together, because we trust in that hour; and it is as though we'd been together the whole day through. If Thanne suffers another sin of mine, it needn't swell in secret until it explodes. The cup is there for it, a place for it, and I drink from the cup, both the medicine that wakens and purges me, and the love with which she nourishes me."[1]

The key for him was an act of his will. He recognized where he had gone wrong and *decided* to do something about it. He came home an hour early every day and spent that hour talking with his wife.

Change of this nature is never easy; in fact, it often feels forced and artificial. Don't despair! In time these changes will bear fruit. For now, they are like seeds planted in the ground of your relationship. There must be a period of germination, followed by a sprouting, before you are finally ready to reap the harvest. In fact, your faithfulness during this "artificial" time will do a great deal to restore trust in the relationship, and as trust grows, your spouse will dare to risk loving you again.

♡♡ *Love in Action*

Identify the changes you need to make in the way you relate to your spouse. Now promise him/her one specific change (e.g. "Every night we'll spend the hour before supper together. I'll be home and we'll talk together").

♡♡ *Thought for the Day*

"...it was not the time with him alone that was important. It was his understanding of her feelings that buoyed her up. It was his attitude that neither his work nor his friends were as important to him as she that gave her the answer she needed."[2]

— H. Norman Wright

♡♡ *Scripture for the Day*

Be kind and compassionate to one another, forgiving each other, just as in Christ God forgave you.

— Ephesians 4:32

♡♡ *Prayer*

Lord, forgive me for being self-centered and insensitive. Grant me a faithful love that I may win my beloved's trust again. In the name of Jesus I pray. Amen.

chapter 45

♡ ♡ ♡ ♡

The Empty Nest

*R*oy and Linda had been married nearly thirty years when their third child, and only daughter, was married in a beautiful wedding, flawlessly choreographed by Linda. As that eventful day wound to a close, Linda's father sought her out. "It was perfect," he said, "from beginning to end." She gave him a wan smile, before taking his hand and leading him to an empty bench.

When they were both seated, he asked, "Is something wrong, Linda?"

Blinking rapidly to keep back her tears, she said, "For the past year I've been consumed with planning Lori's wedding. It's been my life, you might say. But now...." Her voice trailed off.

"What are you trying to say, Linda?" her father asked anxiously.

"Oh, Daddy," she sounded like a little girl again as she let him hug her while she wept soundlessly.

When she had regained her composure, she tried again: "Things aren't the way they used to be. Between Roy and me, I mean. And now that it is just the two of us, I don't know what I am going to do. I don't think I can hide from the truth any longer."

"Have you talked with Roy...about this, I mean?"

"I've tried, Daddy, but he gets that hurt little boy look on his face, and I can't go on. He seems to be so happy, and I don't want to shatter his world." Taking a deep breath, she continued, "I thought I could manage it, and I did pretty well as long as Lori was at home, but now that she's leaving I don't know what I am going to do."

Linda's experience is not uncommon — more acute than most couples' experience, perhaps, but common nonetheless. When the last child leaves home, the dynamics of family life change radically. Needs for communication, affection, and companionship that were once filled, at least in part, by the children must now be met by someone else. Suddenly, a man and his wife are thrown together with no one else to talk to. It's a grand opportunity for intimacy, but for many couples it is threatening. The empty nest becomes a major crisis when two strangers suddenly find themselves alone with each other with the rest of their lives stretching out in front of them.

This is called a predictable crisis, because we know it is going to happen. As surely as children are born, they will grow up and leave the nest. It is part of God's divine plan. Still, that does not make it painless. Under the best of circumstances, it is challenging. Under less than ideal circumstances, it can become a crisis.

Preparing for the empty nest is not complicated, but it is demanding. Nothing is more essential than maintaining an intimate relationship with each other. Private time and deep sharing should be cultivated at all costs. He must guard against becoming overinvolved in his career, and she must be careful not to invest so much of herself in the children that there is nothing left for the marriage.

Be careful not to live as if your children will be with you always. They won't. As they grow up and become increasingly independent, experience your own independence. The empty nest is really a progressive thing. As your children make a few short solo flights, go ahead and deal with your feelings. Don't store them all up for one big crisis.

Accept your new role, rather than grieving over the one you've lost. Your value as a person has not diminished, just changed. Strive to relate to each child as an adult to an adult, rather than a parent to a child. Those who manage this soon discover a rewarding new relationship. They haven't lost a child. They have gained a new friend. The empty nest, like the other predictable crises in marriage, can be an opportunity for enrichment. It's what you make it. The choice is yours.

♡ *Love in Action*

Examine your life and marriage. List the behaviors that give evidence that you are preparing for that day when it will only be the two of you.

♡♡ *Thought for the Day*

"Your children will grow up and leave home. You will eventually retire from your job. Marriage is the only relationship in your life that is until 'death do us part.' Does not wisdom, then, dictate [that you make your relationship with your spouse your number one priority]?"[1]

— Richard Exley

♡♡ *Scripture for the Day*

Your wife will be like a fruitful vine within your house; your sons will be like olive shoots around your table. Thus is the man blessed who fears the LORD.

— Psalm 128:3,4

♡♡ *Prayer*

Lord, bless our empty nest. May the latter years of our marriage be even more blessed than the former years. In the name of Jesus I pray. Amen.

chapter 46

♡ ♡ ♡ ♡

Mid-life Crisis

*O*ne of the reasons mid-life is so hard on a marriage is because a role reversal often occurs: "Men tend to move toward passivity, tenderness and intimacy which they previously repressed. They move toward more expressive ventures and goals. Women tend to become more autonomous, aggressive and cognitive. They now seek more instrumental roles such as a career, money, influence."[1] In short, husbands and wives are moving in opposite directions and often miss each other, passing like ships in the night.

This role reversal, and the resulting crisis, often indicates a weakness in the way many couples relate to their careers and their families. It underlines the futility of a one-dimensional life. The man has invested himself in his career at the expense of his relationship with his family and friends. At mid-life he realizes how unsatisfying that is, and he can't imagine spending the rest of his life so unfulfilled.

The woman, on the other hand, has been a caregiver, nurturing her children and to some degree her husband. Even as her husband is discovering that his career cannot meet all of his emotional needs, she now realizes that living through her family only is not enough either, especially now that the children are grown. In a misguided effort to make a new identity, she often moves away from her husband in search of independence, just when he is turning toward her in search of intimacy. The result — a marriage-threatening mid-life crisis.

Can it be avoided? I think so. Mid-life will always present challenges, but it does not have to be a time of crisis. Concomitant growth is perhaps the single most important factor in preventing a crisis. The man or woman who lives a one-dimensional life is at greater risk than the person who invests himself or herself in a number of areas.

The main cause of a mid-life crisis is the threat to personal identity. Those who sail through this period without apparent trauma are those who have built a varied and solid identity. They see themselves in several roles — spouse, parent, friend, professional, and a person in their own right. Should one of these roles, or identities, be threatened, they are not devastated. They know they are more than just an "accountant" or just a "parent."

In addition, they are expressive persons. They are in touch with their humanity and are willing to share their deepest feelings with those they know and trust. This enables them to establish a social and emotional network, a support system in which they are helped to process their feelings as they occur, rather than denying them for years and then suddenly having to deal with them all at once.

And finally, they are persons who have incorporated the Word of God into their lives. Their confidence is not in temporal things like physical appearance or strength, material wealth or position. They are grounded in the eternal values of God's Word and, as a consequence, they cannot only negotiate change, but thrive on it.

♡ *Love in Action*

As a couple, discuss lifestyle changes that will decrease the risk of a marriage-threatening mid-life crisis. Take specific steps to implement those changes now.

♡ *Thought for the Day*

"I believe that middle-aged marriage, lived as it should be and can be, offers qualities that nothing else has ever superseded: A shelter where two people can grow older without loneliness, the ease of long intimacy, family jokes that don't have to be explained, understanding without words. Most of all it offers memories."[2]

— M. Brown

♡ *Scripture for the Day*

There is a time for everything, and a season for every activity under heaven: a time to be born and a time to die....

— Ecclesiastes 3:1,2

♡ Prayer

Lord, grant us the grace to make peace with mid-life and all it brings. Give us faith to believe that this season, too, can be a time of personal and spiritual growth. In the name of Jesus we pray. Amen.

chapter 47

♡♡♡♡

Cherish the Memories of Yesterday

$\mathcal{B}$renda and I have been married for nearly thirty-one years, and during that time we have put together quite a collection of memories. Some of them are tenderly poignant, like the birth of our daughter Leah. Others are hysterically funny, at least in retrospect. There was the first time we had guests for dinner at the parsonage in Holly, Colorado. Right after we said grace, we heard a splashing noise in the kitchen and discovered a mother mouse and her five babies swimming in the soapy dishwater. Thankfully, our guests were "country folk" and unfazed by it all.

Some of our memories just happened. There is no way we could have planned for the mice, nor would we have wanted to. More often than not, though, our most endearing memories came about as the result of careful planning and considerable forethought. That's not to say you can plan a memory, but you can prepare for it.

One of Brenda's favorite memories is of the week we spent together in a rustic cabin high in the Rockies, immediately following our daughter's wedding. During the day, we picnicked and rode horseback. At night, we read books by kerosene lamp light and reminisced about Leah's childhood, wondering again how it could have slipped away so quickly.

One of my favorite memories is building our cabin in the Ozarks. As a silver anniversary gift to ourselves, Brenda and I purchased 3.5 acres on Beaver Lake in Northwest Arkansas. We christened it Emerald Point because it is situated on a point of land that juts out into brilliant emerald green water. Immediately, we began dreaming of a small cabin where we could get away, a place where I could write without distractions and where our grandchildren (when we have some) could spend time with us.

After nearly two years we were finally ready to begin construction. With an air of excitement we drove onto our property in late March and set up camp. Our friends could hardly believe what we were doing. They simply could not imagine elegant Brenda living in a tent for weeks, while we built our cabin.

As luck would have it, it was one of the wettest springs in history. Night after night the temperatures hovered just above freezing, while an incessant downpour turned our tent into a soggy shelter. Brenda saved the day, or I should say saved the month, with her comic relief.

It's not that she tries to be funny, she just is. Take her improvised sleepwear, for instance. Every night she donned two pairs of thermal underwear, wool socks, and a fur hat that covered her entire head and tied under her chin. The result was hilarious, sending us both into spasms of laughter. After making an outrageous display of modeling her "lingerie" in the damp confines of our frigid tent, she finally joined me under a heaping mound of quilts. When she whispered goodnight, just before blowing out the lantern, I could see her breath. It was that cold! But we were warm beneath the blanket of laughter that echoed softly in the dark.

Now that our cabin is finished we look back and wonder how we did it. I don't think we would try it again, but we wouldn't trade the memories for anything either.

When the tough times come, and believe me they will, you look back at all you've been through together, both the good times and the bad, and you say, "We can make it!" When you are tempted to give up, to wonder if life might not be better if you each went your separate way, you remember all you've shared and you realize that you have too much invested in this relationship to give up now. That's the power of shared memories.

♡♡ Love in Action

Recall two or three special memories of you and your spouse. Plan a special time and place to share those memories together.

♡♡ Thought for the Day

"I remember you, Thanne, in flashes, in frozen images all throughout these eighteen years. It's as though I have snapshots of you on the wall beside me. The times are fixed by the love that shone in them, caught them, and kept them in my memory.

"The more I look at these memories, the more I realize that their radiance is unearthly, though you are no more than an earthly woman. It's a nimbus, Thanne, a divinity. It's a sort of cloud of glory that shines around my remembering and our marriage."[1]

— Walter Wangerin, Jr.

♡♡ Scripture for the Day

You have stolen my heart, my sister, my bride; you have stolen my heart with one glance of your eyes, with one jewel of your necklace.

— Song of Songs 4:9

♡♡ Prayer

Lord, teach us to embrace the joys of our shared past. May these memories become a vision shaping our future together. In the name of Jesus I pray. Amen.

chapter 48

♡ ♡ ♡ ♡

The Gift of Affirmation

$\mathcal{S}$ome time ago, while alone on a ministry trip, I began reminiscing. Like watching slides projected on the screen of my mind, I reviewed the years Brenda and I had spent together. As the memories flashed by, I reached for a yellow legal pad and began jotting them down. I ended up writing Brenda a love letter, recapping the years of our courtship and marriage.

"Brenda," I wrote, "you really are an extraordinary lady, not perfect maybe, but definitely special.

"You are unusually beautiful. We've been married almost thirty-one years, and I still light up when you walk into a room. I'm so proud to be seen with you. Without a doubt I look better when we're together.

"You are gracious and elegant. Under your touch, leftovers become an occasion, and you can turn an ordinary drop-in evening into a festive event. You make cheese and crackers more elegant than caviar. What a joy to bring friends home to our house.

"Remember the Christmas, nearly twenty-eight years ago, when we had no money, and gifts were out of the question? Instead of bemoaning our unhappy plight, we decided to be creative. I remember driving to the river bottom where we collected driftwood and wild flowers. You made your folks an arrangement from a twisted piece of driftwood and dried flowers. From a second piece of driftwood, I made mine a TV lamp, which sits in their bedroom still. Somehow they seem to cherish those homemade gifts above the more expensive, store-bought ones of later years. Maybe it's because love has a way of turning ordinary things into treasures of the heart.

"When the moths invaded us each summer, instead of bemoaning our unhappy plight, you turned a miserable situation into a game. After switching off all the lights, you turned on the gas burners and the kitchen range, frying those dive-bombing bugs!

"No complaints from you, no tearful depressions, not even envy toward those pastors who were faring better than we. You had an amazing ability to be content in all situations. How fortunate I was. How fortunate I am.

"Over the years, you have given me so much, more than I ever imagined possible. Simple things but rare — a quiet place away from the noisy world, a gentle love without demands, inspiration without expectations. Common things too, of uncommon value — a cup of coffee when I come home at night, a fire in the fireplace, supper on the stove.

"I give you me, now and always. I am yours in a way no one else can ever be yours, and in a way I can never be in relationship with anyone else. I will love you all the days of your life. When you are lonely I will comfort you. When you are tired I will refresh you. When you are sick I will care for you.

"I will share all your joys and sorrows your whole life long. We will celebrate growing old together, warmed against winter's chill, by the memories of a lifetime cherished and shared."

There's more, but I think you get the point. I could have called. It would have been far less trouble, but I would not have put the thought and effort into a call that I put into that letter. Besides, it would have been over in a matter of minutes. Brenda can keep the letter for a lifetime.

♡ *Love in Action*

Take a few minutes right now and make a list of the things you most admire about your spouse. Now write her/him a love letter. Be sure you mail it. It will have more impact that way.

♡♡ *Thought for the Day*

"When a husband and wife share their most tender feelings for one another, something almost miraculous happens. Their affirming words become light in a dark place, strength in a moment of weakness, music to the soul. And if their words are reinforced with tender gestures of affection, unexpected kindnesses, and utter dependability, they experience a loving affirmation that enables them to embrace life in ways they never dared alone."[1]

— Richard Exley

♡♡ *Scripture for the Day*

My lover is radiant and ruddy, outstanding among ten thousand.

His head is purest gold; his hair is wavy and black as a raven....

His mouth is sweetness itself; he is altogether lovely. This is my lover, this my friend, O daughters of Jerusalem.

— Song of Songs 5:10,11,16

♡♡ *Prayer*

Lord, give me the gift of affirmation that I may speak words of life to my beloved. In Jesus' name I pray. Amen.

chapter 49

Love for a Lifetime

*S*ome time ago, my father underwent his second bypass surgery. It was an enormously stressful time for all of us, yet in the midst of that crisis I witnessed love as pure and selfless as I ever hope to see. No single act stands out in my mind above the others; rather, it is a mosaic.

I see my mother bending over my father's bed in the intensive care unit reserved for cardiac surgery patients. He is hardly recognizable, resembling not at all the man we kissed good-bye just hours ago. Now his motionless body is fairly entangled with medical devices: a breathing tube, a catheter, a drainage tube, an IV. In addition, he is connected by a complexity of leads to a heart monitor, which records his cardiac functions with squiggly lines on a green-colored screen.

Mother seems not to notice as she bends over him, whispering her love in words he cannot hear. Locating an unencumbered area on his arm, she strokes his skin tenderly. With her other hand, she smoothes his hair down. Standing beside her, I think, "So this is what love looks like after nearly half a century."

Far too soon, a nurse comes and ushers us out, telling us that we can see him again, for fifteen minutes, in three hours.

It is now almost 7:00 P.M., and we have been at the hospital nearly fourteen hours. Although it is a forty-five-minute drive to the folks' house, we decide to go home and rest for a few minutes before returning to the hospital at nine for our allotted quarter-hour visit.

Thus begins a three-day odyssey in which we return to the hospital every three hours so Mother can be with Dad for fifteen minutes. During one of our brief visits, a nurse tells me that she has never seen a more devoted wife. As she walks away, I cannot help thinking of the wedding vows, "...in sickness and in health, to love and to cherish, till death us do part..." Seldom have they seemed so real.

On the third day, as we are about to leave for the hospital, we receive a call informing us that my father has been moved into a private room. Mother is like a schoolgirl in her excitement as she packs a suitcase and prepares to join Dad at the hospital for the duration of his stay. The suitcase she chooses is fairly large, and when I pick it up to take it to the car, I stagger at its weight.

"What do you have in here?" I demand in mock anger.

It turns out that she has packed seven complete outfits for herself, as well as several pairs of pajamas for Dad, and her own nightwear. In addition, she has packed both of their Bibles, a devotional book, *The Pentecostal Evangel*, *Guideposts* and various other reading materials. When I question why she needs so many outfits, she informs me that she is not leaving the hospital until Dad is released. Nor, does she do so until she leaves with him six days later.

I stay one more day, and then I have to catch a flight to take care of my own commitments. Telling Mom and Dad good-bye, I suddenly find myself weeping. For a minute, I do not know why. Dad's prognosis is good, and he is in no immediate danger. Then it hits me. These tears are not for them. They are for me. I am crying because something deep inside me yearns to be loved the way my mother loves my father.

I hear myself praying, "Oh, God, help Brenda to love me like that." Ever so gently, but ever so clearly, the Holy Spirit convicts me, and now I pray, "Oh, God, help me to love Brenda like that."

♡ *Love in Action*

Sit down with your spouse and talk specifically about the kind of relationship you want to have in your later years. Decide together what changes, if any, you need to make in the way you relate to one another.

♡ *Thought for the Day*

"What we do today, good or bad, will become the material out of which we build our future. Unkind words, thoughtless deeds, broken promises, a trust betrayed, will become cornerstones in a marriage haunted by old hurts and present fears. Gentle

words, acts of kindness, a promise kept, a love that is true, these will become the cornerstones in a marriage built by love."[1]

— Richard Exley

♡ Scripture for the Day

A wife of noble character who can find? She is worth far more than rubies. Her husband has full confidence in her and lacks nothing of value. She brings him good, not harm, all the days of her life.

— Proverbs 31:10-12

♡ Prayer

Lord, may I always seek to be loving rather than to be loved. In the name of Jesus I pray. Amen.

chapter 50

♡ ♡ ♡ ♡

The High Cost of Commitment

*I*n March 1990, Dr. Robertson McQuilkin announced his resignation as president of Columbia Bible College, in order to care for his beloved wife, Muriel, who was suffering from the advanced stages of Alzheimer's disease. In his resignation letter he wrote:

"My dear wife, Muriel, has been in failing mental health for about eight years. So far I have been able to carry both her ever-growing needs and my leadership responsibilities at CBC. But recently it has become apparent that Muriel is contented most of the time she is with me and almost none of the time I am away from her. It is not just 'discontent.' She is filled with fear — even terror — that she has lost me and always goes in search of me when I leave home. Then she may be full of anger when she cannot get to me. So it is clear to me that she needs me now, full-time.

"Perhaps it would help you to understand if I shared with you what I shared at the time of the announcement of my resignation in chapel. The decision was made, in a way, 42 years ago when I promised to care for Muriel 'in sickness and in health...till death do us part.' So, as I told the students and faculty, as a man of my word, integrity has something to do with it. But so does fairness. She has cared for me fully and sacrificially all these years; if I cared for her for the next 40 years I would not be out of debt. Duty, however, can be grim and stoic. But there is more; I love Muriel. She is a delight to me — her childlike dependence and confidence in me, her warm love, occasional flashes of that wit I used to relish so, her happy spirit and tough resilience in the face of her continual distressing frustration. I do not have to care for her, I get to! It is a high honor to care for so wonderful a person."[1]

As a man and a husband, I am deeply moved when I read that. Intuitively I realize that's the stuff real marriages are made of — commitment and integrity, for better or for worse. Yet it would be a mistake for us to assume that Dr. McQuilkin's decision was an isolated choice, independent of the hundreds of lesser choices that went into their forty-two years of marriage. In truth, a decision of that magnitude is almost always the culmination of a lifelong series of smaller, daily decisions. And, as such, it challenges every one of us to examine the choices we make each day and the way we relate to our spouse.

♥ *Love in Action*

Determine to find "little" ways to daily lay down your life for your spouse. Do things like giving up Monday night football to spend the evening with her, or giving up a Saturday shopping trip to go fishing with him.

♥ *Thought for the Day*

"...nothing is easier than saying words. Nothing is harder than living them, day after day. What you promise today must be renewed and redecided tomorrow and each day that stretches out before you."[2]

— Arthur Gordon

♥ *Scripture for the Day*

Husbands, love your wives, just as Christ loved the church and gave himself up for her to make her holy, cleansing her by the washing with water through the word, and to present her to himself as a radiant church, without stain or wrinkle or any other blemish, but holy and blameless.

— Ephesians 5:25-27

♥ *Prayer*

Lord, teach me to live and love selflessly day by day so that I will be prepared to lay down my life for my spouse should that day ever come. In the name of Jesus I pray. Amen.

chapter 51
♡♡♡♡

A Love Story

Several years ago, Erich Segal wrote *Love Story*, a tenderly funny and poignant story of two young people who fall in love and marry. It became an instant bestseller and was later made into a movie, but it cannot compare with the real-life love story of the late John and Harriet McCormack.

"They were married fifty-two years and never spent a night apart.... Dr. Billy Graham referred to their marriage as one of the great love stories of our generation. He said there was a very deep spiritual affinity between them that was far more binding than the psychological or the physical. Roger Brooks, their chauffeur of twenty years, declared, 'They were just like newly-weds.'

"Harriet McCormack was eighty-seven years old when she died, and age had worked a cruel toll in her declining years. It had narrowed her vision, and forced her to hide her dark eyes behind glasses. Arthritis, stemming from a leg injury, had slowed her walk to infant steps. Even eating had become a chore, the food had to be soft and in small pieces. Once, at a White House State dinner, John McCormack was observed cutting his wife's meat.

"When Harriet was hospitalized in her eighty-seventh year, John took the hospital room next to hers and kept the door open between them at all times so he could hear her if she called during the night. When she was too warm he bathed her forehead. When she was weak he fed her. When she could no longer eat solid foods, he did not; if she had to endure roast mush, he would endure it with her. In the small hours of the morning her soft moan would come, 'John, John, where are you?' and he would scuffle into his slippers and tug on his bathrobe. 'I'm right here, Harriet, don't worry.' When she slipped into the past, he was not impatient. He went with her. 'I'm so glad I can help her there.' he told John Monohan, 'I can remember her brothers and sisters.'

"He sat there day after day, hour after hour, according to Jo Meegan, and would repeat everything. He would recall all their early life together with great fondness.... When people talked about sacrifice, he scoffed at them. What did they mean? He wanted to be with Harriet. He was annoyed when anyone suggested duty. Duty wasn't love."[1]

Now, I believe with all my heart that this is what God had in mind when He said, "...'It is not good for the man to be alone. I will make a helper suitable for him.'"[2] Yet how few marriages ever approach this divine ideal. Studies indicate that only about 10 percent of all marriages reach their relational potential, the rest struggle along in mediocrity or end in divorce.

♡♡ *Love in Action*

Together, make a list of activities that will help you achieve the full relational potential of your marriage. List things like a weekly date, developing mutual interests, family vacations, and prayer together.

♡♡ *Thought for the Day*

"I guess it's when you love each other the right way, or enough, or something. I think to make a marriage great you have to treat each other like company a lot of the time and be polite and stuff like that!"[3]

— Little girl's essay on "What Makes a Marriage Great?"

♡♡ *Scripture for the Day*

Finally, brothers, whatever is true, whatever is noble, whatever is right, whatever is pure, whatever is lovely, whatever is admirable — if anything is excellent or praiseworthy — think about such things.

— Philippians 4:8

♡♡ *Prayer*

Lord, make our marriage all You intended marriage to be. In the name of Jesus we pray. Amen.

chapter 52
♡ ♡ ♡ ♡

A Kiss for Kate

"Every afternoon when I came on duty as the evening nurse," writes Phyllis Valkins, "I would walk the halls of the nursing home, pausing at each door to chat and observe. Often, Kate and Chris, their big scrapbooks in their laps, would be reminiscing over the photos. Proudly, Kate showed me pictures of by-gone years: Chris — tall, blonde, handsome. Kate — pretty, dark-haired, laughing. Two young lovers smiling through the passing seasons. How lovely they looked now, sitting there, the light shining on their white heads, their time-wrinkled faces smiling at remembrances of the years, caught and held forever in the scrapbooks.

"How little the young know of loving, I'd think. How foolish to think they have a monopoly on such a precious commodity. The old know what loving truly means; the young can only guess.

"Kate and Chris were always together — in the dining room, the lounge, strolling around the big porches and lawns, always holding hands. As we staff members ate our evening meal, sometimes Kate and Chris would walk slowly by the dining-room doors. Then conversation would turn to a discussion of the couple's love and devotion, and what would happen when one of them died.

"Bedtime followed a ritual. When I brought the evening medication, Kate would be sitting in her chair, in nightgown and slippers, awaiting my arrival. Under the watchful eyes of Chris and myself, Kate would take her pill, then carefully Chris would help her from chair to bed and tuck the covers in around her frail body.

"Observing this act of love, I would think for the thousandth time, Good heavens, why don't nursing homes have double beds for married couples? All their lives they have slept together, but in a nursing home, they're expected to sleep in single beds. Overnight they're deprived of a comfort of a lifetime.

"How very foolish such policies are, I would think, as I watched Chris reach up and turn off the light above Kate's bed. Then tenderly he would bend, and they would kiss gently. Chris would pat her cheek, and both would smile. He would pull up the side rail on her bed, and only then would he turn and accept his own medication. As I walked into the hall, I could hear Chris say, 'Good-night, Kate,' and her returning voice, 'Good-night, Chris,' while the space of an entire room separated their two beds.

"I had been off duty two days and when I returned, the first news I heard was, 'Chris died yesterday morning.'

"'How?'

"'A heart attack. It happened quickly.'

"'How's Kate?'

"'Bad.'

"We pampered Kate for awhile, letting her eat in her room, surrounding her with special attention. Then gradually the staff worked her back into the old schedule. Often, as I went past her room, I would observe Kate sitting in her chair, scrapbooks on her lap, gazing sadly at pictures of Chris.

Bedtime was the worst part of the day for Kate. Although she had been granted her request to move from her bed to Chris's bed, and although the staff chatted and laughed with her as they tucked her in for the night, still Kate remained silent and sadly withdrawn. Passing her room an hour after she had been tucked in, I'd find her wide awake, staring at the ceiling.

"The weeks passed, and bedtime wasn't any better. She seemed so restless, so insecure. Why? I wondered. Why this time of day more than the other hours?

"Then one night as I walked into her room, only to find the same wide-awake Kate, I said impulsively, 'Kate, could it be you miss your good-night kiss?' Bending down, I kissed her wrinkled cheek.

"It was as though I had opened the floodgates. Tears coursed down her face, her hands gripped mine. 'Chris always kissed me good-night,' she cried. 'I know,' I whispered.

"'I miss him so, all those years he kissed me good-night.' She paused while I wiped the tears. 'I just can't seem to go to sleep without his kiss.'

"She looked up at me, eyes brimming. 'Oh, thank you for giving me a kiss.'

"A small smile turned up the corners of her mouth. 'You know,' she said confidentially, 'Chris used to sing me a song.'

"'He did?' 'Yes' — her white head nodded — 'and I lie here at night and think about it.'

"'How did it go?'

"Kate smiled, held my hand and cleared her throat. Then her voice, small with age, but still melodious, lifted softly in song: 'So kiss me, my sweet, and so let us part. And when I grow too old to dream, that kiss will live in my heart.'"[1]

♡♡ *Love in Action*

If your marriage were to continue on its present course for the next thirty years, what kind of relationship would you have? Would it be characterized by kindness and affection? Or would it be plagued by loneliness and bitterness?

♡♡ *Thought for the Day*

"*Come grow old with me.*
The best is yet to be."

— Robert Browning

♡♡ Scripture for the Day

A wife of noble character who can find? She is worth far more than rubies. Her husband has full confidence in her and lacks nothing of value. She brings him good, not harm, all the days of her life.

— Proverbs 31:10-12

♡♡ Prayer

Lord, may we grow old together, warmed against winter's chill by the memories of a lifetime, cherished and shared. In Your Holy name we pray. Amen.

chapter 53

♡ ♡ ♡ ♡

The Gift of Forgiveness

*I*t is December 24, 1988, and for the first time ever Brenda and I are celebrating Christmas alone. Determining to make the best of it, I build a fire in the fireplace and light the kerosene lamps on the mantle while Brenda prepares eggnog in the kitchen.

After a bit, she comes to join me in front of the fire, but instead of sitting beside me on the love seat, she kneels behind me and puts both arms around my neck. "I have something for you," she says, handing me a red envelope.

"A Christmas card," I think, "how nice." Then I see a hand-written note beneath the printed verse. As I begin to read it, my eyes grow misty, and my throat aches, so great is the lump that forms there.

In an instant, I am transported back to a Sunday afternoon in August nearly ten years earlier. We are quarreling as we have done numerous times before during our thirteen-year marriage. I've long since forgotten what started it, some insignificant thing most likely, but it soon turns deadly.

And then Brenda speaks the words that seem to seal my fate. "I hate you," she sobs. "I hate you! I can't live this way. I won't. When Leah graduates, I am going to divorce you."

Stumbling beneath the awful weight of her terrible pain, she flees the room, leaving an unbearable emptiness in her wake. I hear the bathroom door close, then lock. A heavy sadness envelopes me. Never have I felt so alone, so helpless.

Descending the stairs toward my study, I try to convince myself that Brenda doesn't really mean what she said. She is just angry. She wouldn't really divorce me. Surely not.

Like a zombie, I go through the motions of preparing a sermon for the evening service. But my mind is grappling with weightier matters. What will I do if Brenda really does leave me when Leah graduates? How will I cope? I truly love her, even if she cannot imagine that I do. And I can change. I will show her.

Yet, even in the aftermath of the revelation of how my anger is destroying her, I am tempted to rationalize, to somehow justify my behavior. I am not a bad man. I compliment Brenda often and express my love to her every day. I am affectionate, appreciative, and I never forget her birthday or our anniversary. I write her poems and take her out to dinner. Doesn't that count for something?

We never speak of that tragic Sunday afternoon again. But for years, nine years and four months to be exact, that painful moment lies like a piece of misplaced furniture in the soul of our relationship. Any time we try to get close to each other, we bump into it.

As the years pass, things seem to improve between us. Many a night I lie on the bed watching Brenda as she prepares to join me and think how blessed we are. Not infrequently I ask her, "Do you think anyone is as happy as we are?" Giving me a quick smile and a hug, before turning out the light, she says, "I'm sure there are others just as happy."

Lying in the darkness, I think, "It's going to be all right. She's happier now, I can tell." But oh, how I long to hear her say, "Richard, all is forgiven. I don't hate you any more. I love you." I can't ask though, lest I awaken her old hurts. I can only wait. And hope.

In May 1988, Leah graduates from high school and leaves home to begin a life of her own. Now it is just the two of us. June turns into December, and before we hardly know it, it is Christmas Eve....

Straining to make out Brenda's words through tear-blurred eyes, I return to the present. Haltingly, I read: "I Brenda Starr take thee Richard Dean to be my lawfully wedded husband. To have and to hold from this day forward. For richer, for poorer, in sickness and in health, till death do us part. To love, honor, cherish and obey. Forsaking all others and thereto I plight thee my troth. In the name of the Father, the Son and the Holy Ghost.

"It looks like you're stuck with me! I'm not going anywhere! Always remember 'I'll never leave thee nor forsake thee.'

Your Devoted Wife & Lover,
Brenda Starr"

All at once I am undone, overwhelmed, by such mercy and grace. Turning to Brenda I crush her to my chest. The awful burden of ten long years is lifted. The dark cloud of condemnation is dissipated. That misplaced piece of furniture is gone. There is nothing between us. In the soul of our marriage there is only love, and we are one.

♡ *Love in Action*

Examine your marriage and see if you have made any mistakes that you have not been willing to own. If there are any, specifically identify them now and honestly confess them to your spouse.

Now examine your marriage and see if you are harboring any unforgiveness toward your spouse. If so, determine right now that you are going to forgive him/her.

♡ *Thought for the Day*

"How often had we hugged before? I can't count the times. How good had those hugs been? I couldn't measure the goodness. But this hug — don't you know, it was my salvation, different from any other and more remarkable because this is the hug I should never have had. That is forgiveness! The law was gone. Rights were all abandoned. Mercy took their place. We were

married again. And it was you, Christ Jesus, in my arms —
within my graceful Thanne. One single, common hug, and we
were alive again."[1]

— Walter Wangerin, Jr.

♥♥ Scripture for the Day

Get rid of all bitterness, rage and anger.... Be kind and
compassionate to one another, forgiving each other, just as in
Christ God forgave you.

— Ephesians 4:31,32

♥♥ Prayer

Lord, I have been given a second chance, a new beginning.
With Your help I will make the most of it. I will love my spouse
all the days of my life, and together we will build a marriage
that lasts. In the name of Jesus I pray. Amen.

ENDNOTES

Preface
[1]Proverbs 19:14

Chapter 2
[1]Desmond Morris, *Intimate Behavior* (New York: Random House, 1971), p. 73.

Chapter 3
[1]Charlie W. Shedd, *Letters to Karen* (Nashville: Abingdon Press, 1965), pp. 23, 24.

Chapter 4
[1]Dr. Frank and Mary Alice Minirth, Dr. Brian and Dr. Deborah Newman, Dr. Robert and Susan Hemfelt, *Passages of Marriage* (Nashville: Thomas Nelson Publishers, 1991), pp. 18,19.

Chapter 5
[1]Walter Wangerin, Jr., *As for Me and My House* (Nashville: Thomas Nelson Publishers, 1987), pp. 30,31.

Chapter 6
[1]Charlie W. Shedd, *Letters to Philip* (New York: Doubleday & Company, Inc., 1968), p. 91.

Chapter 7
[1]Charlie W. Shedd, *Letters to Karen* (Nashville: Abingdon Press, 1965).
[2]Charlie W. Shedd, *Letters to Philip* (Garden City: Doubleday & Company, Inc., 1968).
[3]Rich Buhler, "Learning the Language of Love," quoted in *The Making of a Marriage* (Nashville: Thomas Nelson Publishers, 1993), p. 82.

Chapter 8

[1]Dorothy T. Samuel, *Fun and Games in Marriage* (Waco: Word Books Publisher, 1973), p. 21.

[2]Dr. James Dobson, *Dr. Dobson Answers Your Questions* (Wheaton: Tyndale House Publishers, 1982), p. 329.

[3]Dorothy T. Samuel, *Fun and Games in Marriage* (Waco: Word Books Publisher, 1973), p. 23.

Chapter 10

[1]Harold Kushner, *Who Needs God?* (New York: Summit Books, 1989), pp. 4-12.

[2]Madeleine L'Engle, "Walking on Water," quoted in *Disciplines for the Inner Life* by Bob Benson and Michael W. Benson (Waco: Word Book Publishers, 1985), p. 309.

Chapter 11

[1]Charlie W. Shedd, *Letters to Karen* (Nashville: Abingdon Press, 1965), p. 13.

Chapter 12

[1]Dale Carnegie, quoted in *Dawnings*, edited by Phyllis Hobe (Waco: Word Books Publisher, 1981), p. 196.

[2]Proverbs 5:18,19.

[3]Aletha Jane Lindstrom, "A Legacy of Rainbows," *Reader's Digest,* December 1984, p. 122.

[4]Walter Wangerin, Jr., *As for Me and My House* (Nashville: Thomas Nelson Publishers, 1987), pp. 248,249.

Chapter 13

[1]Dr. James Dobson, *What Wives Wish Their Husbands Knew About Women* (Wheaton: Tyndale House Publishers, Inc., 1975), p. 117.

Chapter 14

[1]Ann Landers, "New Rules for the Marriage Game," *Family Circle,* February 3, 1981.

[2]Genesis 2:20.
[3]Genesis 2:22,25.
[4]Lois Wyse, *Love Poems for the Very Married* (Cleveland: World Publishing Co., 1967), p. 45.

Chapter 15
[1]John 8:32.
[2]Genesis 1:27,28,31.
[3]Genesis 2:22,25.
[4]Hebrews 13:4 KJV.
[5]Walter Wangerin, Jr., *As for Me and My House* (Nashville: Thomas Nelson Publishers, 1987), p. 175.

Chapter 16
[1]Dr. James Dobson, *What Wives Wish Their Husbands Knew About Women* (Wheaton: Tyndale House Publishers, Inc., 1975), p. 127.

Chapter 17
[1]Richard Exley, *Marriage in the Making* (Tulsa: Honor Books, 1994), p. 56.

Chapter 18
[1]John Steinbeck, *Of Mice and Men* (New York: A Bantam Book published by arrangement with The Viking Press, Inc., 1971), pp. 79,80.
[2]Genesis 2:25.
[3]C. S. Lewis, quoted by Paul D. Robbins in "Must Men Be Friendless?" *Leadership,* Fall Quarter, 1984, p. 28.
[4]Walter Wangerin, Jr., *As for Me and My House* (Nashville: Thomas Nelson Publishers, 1987), p. 58.

Chapter 19
[1]Dave and Claudia Arp, "Learning to Say the 'S' Word or Building a Creative Love Life," taken from *The Marriage*

Track and quoted in *The Making of a Marriage* (Nashville: Thomas Nelson Publishers, 1993), p. 178.

[2]Walter Wangerin, Jr., *As for Me and My House* (Nashville: Thomas Nelson Publishers, 1987), pp. 112,113.

Chapter 20

[1]Charlie W. Shedd, *Letters to Philip* (Garden City: Doubleday & Company, Inc., 1968), p. 94.

Chapter 21

[1]M. Scott Peck, M.D., *Meditations from the Road* (New York: Simon & Schuster, A Touchstone Book, 1993), p. 312.

Chapter 22

[1]David Mace, *Love and Anger in Marriage* (Grand Rapids: Zondervan Publishing House, 1982), p. 12.

[2]Howard J. Clinebell and Charlotte H. Clinebell, *The Intimate Marriage* (New York: Harper & Row Publishers, 1970), p. 98.

[3]*Ibid.*

[4]M. Scott Peck, M.D., *Meditations from the Road* (New York: Simon & Schuster, A Touchstone Book, 1993), p. 56.

Chapter 23

[1]Howard J. Clinebell and Charlotte H. Clinebell, *The Intimate Marriage* (New York: Harper & Row Publishers, Inc., 1970), p. 98.

Chapter 24

[1]H. Norman Wright, *Communication: Key to Your Marriage* (Ventura: Regal Books, 1974), p. 145.

[2]Ephesians 4:26,27.

Chapter 25

[1]Joshua 24:15.

Chapter 26

[1] H. Norman Wright, *Seasons of a Marriage* (Ventura: Regal Books, 1982), p. 42.

Chapter 27

[1] H. Norman Wright, *Seasons of a Marriage* (Ventura: Regal Books, 1982), pp. 40,41.

Chapter 28

[1] Richard Exley, *Blue-Collar Christianity* (Tulsa: Honor Books, 1989), p. 146.

Chapter 29

[1] Ken Gire, *Windows of the Soul* (Grand Rapids: Zondervan Publishing House, 1996), pp. 208,209.

Chapter 30

[1] Dave and Claudia Arp, "Learning to Say the 'S' Word or Building a Creative Love Life," taken from *The Marriage Track* and quoted in *The Making of a Marriage* (Nashville: Thomas Nelson Publishers, 1993), p. 175.

Chapter 32

[1] Pat Conroy, *The Prince of Tides* (Boston: Houghton Mifflin Company, 1986), p. 23.
[2] Richard Exley, *Life's Bottom Line* (Tulsa: Honor Books, 1990), p. 122.

Chapter 33

[1] Frederick Herwaldt, Jr., "The Ideal Relationship and Other Myths About Marriage," *Christianity Today*, April 9, 1982, p. 30.

Chapter 34

[1] Walter Wangerin, Jr., *As for Me and My House* (Nashville: Thomas Nelson Publishers, 1987), p. 79.

Chapter 35
[1]K. C. Cole, "Playing Together: From Couples That Play," *Psychology Today*, February 1982.
[2]Richard Exley, *Blue-Collar Christianity* (Tulsa: Honor Books, 1989), p. 91.

Chapter 36
[1]Paul Tournier, *To Understand Each Other*, translated by John S. Gilmour (Richmond: John Knox Press, 1962), p. 51.

Chapter 37
[1]Proverbs 6:27-29,32.
[2]R. Kent Hughes, *Disciplines of a Godly Man* (Wheaton: Crossway Books, 1991), p. 32.

Chapter 38
[1]Walter Wangerin, Jr., *As for Me and My House* (Nashville: Thomas Nelson Publishers, 1987), pp. 196,197.
[2]*Ibid.*, p. 195.
[3]Thomas à Kempis, *Imitation of Christ*, quoted in *Habitation of Dragons* by Keith Miller (Waco: Word Books Publisher, 1970), p. 110.

Chapter 40
[1]Walter Wangerin, Jr., *As for Me and My House* (Nashville: Thomas Nelson Publishers, 1987), pp. 88,89.

Chapter 41
[1]David Augsburger, *Caring Enough to Forgive* (Ventura: Regal Books, 1981), pp. 50,57.

Chapter 42
[1]Henry A. Virkler, Ph.D., *Broken Promises* (Dallas: Word Books Publisher, 1992), p. 240.

Chapter 43
[1]Dr. David Stoop and Jan Stoop, "Nine Myths About Intimacy," quoted in *The Making of a Marriage* (Nashville: Thomas Nelson Publishers, 1993), p. 69.

Chapter 44
[1]Walter Wangerin, Jr., *As for Me and My House* (Nashville: Thomas Nelson Publishers, 1987), pp. 110,111.
[2]H. Norman Wright, *Seasons of a Marriage* (Ventura: Regal Books, 1982), p. 98.

Chapter 45
[1]Richard Exley, *Marriage in the Making* (Tulsa: Honor Books, 1994), p. 174.

Chapter 46
[1]H. Norman Wright, *Seasons of a Marriage* (Ventura: Regal Books, 1982), p. 57.
[2]M. Brown, "Keeping Marriage Alive Through the Middle Age," *McCall's*, January, 1973, p. 73.

Chapter 47
[1]Walter Wangerin, Jr., *As for Me and My House* (Nashville: Thomas Nelson Publishers, 1987), pp. 248,249.

Chapter 48
[1]Richard Exley, *Marriage in the Making* (Tulsa: Honor Books, 1994), p. 154.

Chapter 49
[1]Richard Exley, *Straight from the Heart for Couples* (Tulsa: Honor Books, 1995), p. 69.

Chapter 50
[1]R. Kent Hughes, *Disciplines of a Godly Man* (Wheaton: Crossway Books, 1991), pp. 35,36.
[2]Arthur Gordon, *A Touch of Wonder* (Old Tappan: Fleming H. Revell Company, 1974), p. 20.

Chapter 51

[1] Peggy Stanton, *The Daniel Dilemma* (Waco: Word Books Publisher, 1978), pp. 41,43,57.

[2] Genesis 2:18.

[3] Charlie W. Shedd, *Letters to Karen* (Nashville: Abingdon Press, 1965), p. 40.

Chapter 52

[1] Phyllis Valkins, "A Kiss for Kate," *Reader's Digest*, August 1982, condensed from *The Denver Post*.

Chapter 53

[1] Walter Wangerin, Jr., *As for Me and My House* (Nashville: Thomas Nelson Publishers, 1987), pp. 90,91.

Other books by Richard Exley
— available at your local bookstore.

...And Then He Called My Name
Straight From the Heart for Mom
Straight From the Heart for Dad
Straight From the Heart for Couples
Straight From the Heart for Graduates
A Touch of Christmas
How to Be a Man of Character in a World of Compromise
Marriage in the Making
The Making of a Man
Blue-Collar Christianity
Life's Bottom Line
Perils of Power
The Rhythm of Life
When You Lose Someone You Love
The Other God — Seeing God as He Really Is
The Painted Parable